Richard J. Maybury's
Uncle Eric Books

Review Comments or Endorsements
about Current or Previous Editions of the Uncle Eric Books

"None of my kids are graduating from high school until they've finished reading all these books. Very highly recommended." (5 hearts)
—Mary Pride
PRACTICAL HOMESCHOOLING MAGAZINE

"Uncle Eric is on my top 10 list of homeschool resources."
-William Cormier
Freelance writer and homeschool dad

"San Francisco Independent Scholars would like to encourage all students to expand their understanding of economics by reading one or more of these excellent books: WHATEVER HAPPENED TO JUSTICE?, WHATEVER HAPPENED TO PENNY CANDY?, THE MONEY MYSTERY, THE CLIPPER SHIP STRATEGY."
-2002 SFIS Economics Essay Competition

"Richard Maybury's new book, THE CLIPPER SHIP STRATEGY, is an outstanding addition to his series dealing with the subjects of economics, law, politics, business and freedom. His extraordinary ability to present complex subjects in simple, common-sense terms, spiced with humor and fascinating examples, makes this book and the others in the series must reading for both the young and adults, alike. In fact, the entire series should be a required, integral, component of the social studies curriculum in all public and private schools. This would bring a quantum leap upward in the quality of citizenship in this country in a single generation."
—William P. Snavely
Emeritus Professor of Economics
George Mason University

"Like our previous Maybury favorites, WHATEVER HAPPENED TO PENNY CANDY? and WHATEVER HAPPENED TO JUSTICE?, in ARE YOU LIBERAL? CONSERVATIVE? OR CONFUSED? Uncle Eric leaps to the rescue, firing off 26 thoroughly fascinating letters on political philosophies, past, present, and future. The book is recommended for readers aged 14 and up, but I'd crank it down a few years — Uncle Eric is clear as a bell."
—Becky Rupp, Author and Reviewer
"Good Stuff," HOME EDUCATION MAGAZINE

About the Uncle Eric Series

The Uncle Eric series of books is written by Richard J. Maybury for young and old alike. Using the epistolary style of writing (using letters to tell a story), Mr. Maybury plays the part of an economist writing a series of letters to his niece or nephew. Using stories and examples, he gives interesting and clear explanations of topics that are generally thought to be too difficult for anyone but experts.

Mr. Maybury warns, "beware of anyone who tells you a topic is above you or better left to experts. Many people are twice as smart as they think they are, but they've been intimidated into believing some topics are above them. You can understand almost anything if it is explained well."

The series is called UNCLE ERIC'S MODEL OF HOW THE WORLD WORKS. In the series, Mr. Maybury writes from the political, legal and economic viewpoint of America's Founders. The books can be read in any order, and have been written to stand alone. To get the most from each one, however, Mr. Maybury suggests the following order of reading:

Uncle Eric's Model
of How the World Works

Uncle Eric Talks About Personal, Career, and Financial Security

Whatever Happened to Penny Candy?

Whatever Happened to Justice?

Are You Liberal? Conservative? or Confused?

Ancient Rome: How It Affects You Today

Evaluating Books: What Would Thomas Jefferson Think About This?

The Money Mystery

The Clipper Ship Strategy

The Thousand Year War in the Mideast

World War I: The Rest of the Story and How It Affects You Today

World War II: The Rest of the Story and How It Affects You Today

(Study guides available or forthcoming for above titles.)

An Uncle Eric Book

Uncle Eric Talks About Personal, Career, and Financial Security

Second Edition
Extensively Revised and Expanded

by **Richard J. Maybury**
(Uncle Eric)

published by
Bluestocking Press
www.BluestockingPress.com

Printed and bound in the United States of America.
Cover design by Brian C. Williams, El Dorado, CA
Edited by Jane A. Williams and Kathryn Daniels
ISBN 0-942617-38-X

Library of Congress Cataloging-in-Publication Data

Maybury, Rick.
    Uncle Eric talks about personal, career, and financial security / by Richard J. Maybury (Uncle Eric); edited by Jane A. Williams and Kathryn Daniels.-- 2nd ed., extensively revised and expanded.
        p. cm. -- (An Uncle Eric book)
    Includes bibliographical references and index.
    ISBN 0-942617-38-X (alk. paper)
    1. Economics--Study and teaching--Juvenile literature. 2. Law--Study and teaching--Juvenile literature. 3. Children--Vocational guidance--United States--Juvenile literature. 4. Entrepreneurship--Juvenile literature. 5. Financial security--Juvenile literature. I. Williams, Jane A., 1950- II. Daniels, Kathryn Ann. III. Title.

HB74.5.M39 2004
332.024--dc22   2004000121

Published by Bluestocking Press • P.O. Box 1014
Placerville, CA 95667-1014
web site: www.BluestockingPress.com

To my editor, Jane Williams, who deserves a Medal of Honor for fighting the war for liberty more intelligently and tenaciously than anyone I have ever heard of.

> **"...the entire [Uncle Eric] series should be a required, integral, component of the social studies curriculum in all public and private schools. This would bring a quantum leap upward in the quality of citizenship in this country in a single generation."**
>
> **—William P. Snavely**
> **Emeritus Professor of Economics**
> **George Mason University**

Uncle Eric's Model
of How the World Works

What is a model? In his book UNCLE ERIC TALKS ABOUT PERSONAL, CAREER, AND FINANCIAL SECURITY, Richard Maybury (Uncle Eric) explains that one of the most important things you can teach children or learn yourself is:

"Models are how we think, they are how we understand how the world works. As we go through life we build these very complex pictures in our minds of how the world works, and we're constantly referring back to them — matching incoming data against our models. That's how we make sense of things.

"One of the most important uses for models is in sorting incoming information to decide if it's important or not.

"In most schools, models are never mentioned because the teachers are unaware of them. One of the most dangerous weaknesses in traditional education is that it contains no model for political history. Teachers teach what they were taught—and no one ever mentioned models to them, so they don't teach them to their students.

"For the most part, children are just loaded down with collections of facts that they are made to memorize. Without good models, children have no way to know which facts are important and which are not. Students leave school thinking history is a senseless waste of time. Then, deprived of the real lessons of history, the student is vulnerable.

The question is, which models to teach. Mr. Maybury says, "The two models that I think are crucially important for everyone to learn are economics and law."

WHATEVER HAPPENED TO PENNY CANDY? explains the economic model, which is based on Austrian economics, the most free-market of all economic models. WHATEVER HAPPENED TO JUSTICE? explains the legal model and shows the connection between rational law and economic progress. The legal model is the old British Common Law — or Natural Law. The original principles on which America was founded were those of the old British Common Law.

These two books, PENNY CANDY and JUSTICE, provide the overall model of how human civilization works, especially the world of money.

Once the model is understood, read ARE YOU LIBERAL? CONSERVATIVE? OR CONFUSED? This book explains political philosophies relative to Uncle Eric's Model — and makes a strong case for consistency to that model, no exceptions.

Next, read ANCIENT ROME: HOW IT AFFECTS YOU TODAY, which shows what happens when a society ignores Uncle Eric's Model and embraces fascism—an all too common practice these days, although the word fascism is never used.

To help you locate books and authors generally in agreement with these economic and legal models, Mr. Maybury wrote EVALUATING BOOKS: WHAT WOULD THOMAS JEFFERSON THINK ABOUT THIS? This book provides guidelines for selecting books that are consistent with the principles of America's Founders. You can apply these guidelines to books, movies, news commentators, and current events — to any spoken or written medium.

Further expanding on the economic model, THE MONEY MYSTERY explains the hidden force affecting your career, business, and investments. Some economists refer to this force as velocity, others to money demand. Whichever term is used, it is one of the least understood forces affecting your life. Knowing about velocity and money demand not only gives you an understanding of history that few others have, it prepares you to understand and avoid pitfalls in your career, business, and investments. THE MONEY MYSTERY is the first sequel to WHATEVER HAPPENED TO PENNY CANDY? It provides essential background for getting the most from THE CLIPPER SHIP STRATEGY.

THE CLIPPER SHIP STRATEGY explains how government's interference in the economy affects business, careers, and investments. It's a practical nuts-and-bolts strategy for prospering in our turbulent economy. This book is the second sequel to WHATEVER HAPPENED TO PENNY CANDY? and should be read after THE MONEY MYSTERY.

THE THOUSAND YEAR WAR IN THE MIDEAST: HOW IT AFFECTS YOU TODAY explains how events on the other side of the world a thousand years ago can affect us more than events in our own hometowns today. In the last quarter of the 20th century, the Thousand Year War has been the cause of great shocks to the investment markets — the oil embargoes, the Iranian hostage crisis, the Iraq-Kuwait war, the Caucasus Wars over the Caspian Sea oil basin, and September 11, 2001 — and it is likely to remain so for decades to come. Forewarned is forearmed. You must understand where this war is leading to manage your career, business, and investments.

The explosion of the battleship Maine in Havana Harbor in 1898 was the beginning of a chain reaction that eventually led to the destruction of the World Trade Center. In his two-part World War series Richard Maybury explains that an unbroken line leads directly from the Spanish-American War through World War I, World War II, the Korean and Vietnam Wars, the Iraq-Kuwait War, and the "War on Terror" that began September 11, 2001. Mr. Maybury explains the other side of the story, the side you are not likely to get anywhere else, in this two-part World War series: WORLD WAR I: THE REST OF THE STORY AND HOW IT AFFECTS YOU TODAY and WORLD WAR II: THE REST OF THE STORY AND HOW IT AFFECTS YOU TODAY.

Uncle Eric's Model
of How the World Works

These books can be read in any order and have been written to stand alone. But to get the most from each one, Mr. Maybury suggests the following order of reading:

Book 1. UNCLE ERIC TALKS ABOUT PERSONAL, CAREER, AND FINANCIAL SECURITY.

Uncle Eric's Model introduced. Models (or paradigms) are how people think; they are how we understand our world. To achieve success in our careers, investments, and every other part of our lives, we need sound models. These help us recognize and use the information that is important and bypass that which is not. In this book, Mr. Maybury introduces the model he has found most useful. These are explained in WHATEVER HAPPENED TO PENNY CANDY? WHATEVER HAPPENED TO JUSTICE? and THE CLIPPER SHIP STRATEGY.
(Study Guide available.)

Book 2.   WHATEVER HAPPENED TO PENNY CANDY? A FAST,
CLEAR, AND FUN EXPLANATION OF THE ECONOMICS YOU
NEED FOR SUCCESS IN YOUR CAREER, BUSINESS, AND
INVESTMENTS.
The economic model explained. The clearest and
most interesting explanation of economics around.
Learn about investment cycles, velocity, business
cycles, recessions, inflation, money demand, and
more. Contains "Beyond the Basics," which
supplements the basic ideas and is included for
readers who choose to tackle more challenging
concepts. Recommended by former U.S. Treasury
Secretary William Simon and many others.
(Study Guide available.)

Book 3.   WHATEVER HAPPENED TO JUSTICE?
The legal model explained. Explores America's
legal heritage. Shows what is wrong with our legal
system and economy, and how to fix it. Discusses
the difference between higher law and man-made
law, and the connection between rational law and
economic prosperity. Introduces the Two Laws:
1) Do all you have agreed to do. 2) Do not
encroach on other persons or their property.
(Study Guide available.)

Book 4.   ARE YOU LIBERAL? CONSERVATIVE? OR CONFUSED?
Political labels. What do they mean? Liberal,
conservative, left, right, democrat, republican,
moderate, socialist, libertarian, communist —
what are their economic policies, and what plans
do their promoters have for your money? Clear,
concise explanations. Facts and fallacies.
(Study Guide available.)

Book 5.   ANCIENT ROME: HOW IT AFFECTS YOU TODAY.
This book explains what happens when a society ignores the model. Are we heading for fascism like ancient Rome? Mr. Maybury uses historical events to explain current events, including the wars in the former Soviet Empire, and the legal and economic problems of America today. With the turmoil in Russia and Russia's return to fascism, you must read this book to understand your future. History does repeat.
(Study Guide available.)

Book 6.   EVALUATING BOOKS: WHAT WOULD THOMAS JEFFERSON THINK ABOUT THIS?
Most books, magazines, and news stories are slanted against the principles of America's Founders. Often the writers are not aware of it, they simply write as they were taught. Learn how to identify the bias so you can make informed reading, listening, and viewing choices.

Book 7.   THE MONEY MYSTERY: THE HIDDEN FORCE AFFECTING YOUR CAREER, BUSINESS, AND INVESTMENTS.
The first sequel to WHATEVER HAPPENED TO PENNY CANDY? Some economists refer to velocity, others to money demand. However it is seen, it is one of the least understood forces affecting our businesses, careers, and investments — it is the financial trigger. This book discusses precautions you should take and explains why Federal Reserve officials remain so afraid of inflation. THE MONEY MYSTERY prepares you to understand and avoid pitfalls in your career, business, and investments.
(Study Guide available.)

Book 8.   THE CLIPPER SHIP STRATEGY: FOR SUCCESS IN YOUR CAREER, BUSINESS, AND INVESTMENTS.

The second sequel to WHATEVER HAPPENED TO PENNY CANDY? Conventional wisdom says that when the government expands the money supply, the money descends on the economy in a uniform blanket. This is wrong. The money is injected into specific locations causing hot spots or "cones" such as the tech bubble of the 1990s. Mr. Maybury explains his system for tracking and profiting from these cones. Practical nuts-and-bolts strategy for prospering in our turbulent economy. *(Study Guide available.)*

Book 9.   THE THOUSAND YEAR WAR IN THE MIDEAST: HOW IT AFFECTS YOU TODAY.

Mr. Maybury shows that events on the other side of the world a thousand years ago can affect us more than events in our hometowns today. This book explains the ten-century battle the U.S. has entered against the Islamic world. It predicted the events that began unfolding on September 11, 2001. It helps you understand the thinking of the Muslims in the Mideast, and why the coming oil war will affect investment markets around the globe. In the last three decades this war has been the cause of great shocks to the economy and investment markets, including the oil embargoes, the Iranian hostage crisis, the Iraq-Kuwait war, the Caucasus Wars over the Caspian Sea oil basin, and the September 11th attack — and it is likely to remain so for decades to come. Forewarned is forearmed. To successfully manage your career, business, and investments, you must understand this war. *(Contact Bluestocking Press regarding Study Guide availability.)*

Book 10. WORLD WAR I: THE REST OF THE STORY AND HOW IT AFFECTS YOU TODAY, 1870 TO 1935.
The explosion of the battleship Maine in Havana Harbor in 1898 was the beginning of a chain reaction that continues today. Mr. Maybury presents an idea-based explanation of the First World War. He focuses on the ideas and events that led to World War I, events during the war, and how they led to World War II. Includes the ten deadly ideas that lead to war. *(Contact Bluestocking Press regarding Study Guide availability.)*

Book 11. WORLD WAR II: THE REST OF THE STORY AND HOW IT AFFECTS YOU TODAY, 1935 TO SEPTEMBER 11, 2001.
An idea-based explanation of the war. Focuses on events in the Second World War and how our misunderstanding of this war led to America's subsequent wars, including the Korean and Vietnam Wars, the Iraq-Kuwait War, and the "War on Terror" that began September 11, 2001. *(Contact Bluestocking Press regarding Study Guide availability.)*

Reviewer's comments or endorsements of the Uncle Eric books are listed after the Index of this book.

Quantity Discounts Available

The Uncle Eric books are available at special quantity discounts for bulk purchases to individuals, businesses, schools, libraries, and associations, to be distributed as gifts, premiums, or as fund raisers.

For terms and discount schedule contact:

Special Sales Department
Bluestocking Press
Phone: 800-959-8586
email: CustomerService@BluestockingPress.com
web site: www.BluestockingPress.com

Specify how books are to be distributed: for classrooms, or as gifts, premiums, fund raisers — or to be resold.

Study Guide Available

A BLUESTOCKING GUIDE:
BUILDING A PERSONAL MODEL FOR SUCCESS
by Jane A. Williams

— based on Richard J. Maybury's book —
UNCLE ERIC TALKS ABOUT PERSONAL, CAREER, AND
FINANCIAL SECURITY

A BLUESTOCKING GUIDE: BUILDING A PERSONAL MODEL FOR SUCCESS is designed to enhance a student's understanding and retention of the subject matter presented in the corresponding primer: UNCLE ERIC TALKS ABOUT PERSONAL, CAREER, AND FINANCIAL SECURITY.

The study guide includes comprehension questions and answers (relating to specific chapters within the primer), application questions (to guide the student in applying the concepts learned to everyday life), and a final exam. Also included are research and essay assignments, as well as thought questions to facilitate student-instructor discussion. Some suggestions for further reading and/or viewing are also listed.

Order from your favorite book store or direct from the publisher: Bluestocking Press (see order information on last page of this book).

Study Guides
are available or forthcoming
for other Uncle Eric books.

Contents

Note to Reader

Throughout the book, beginning with Chapter One, when a word that appears in the glossary is introduced in the text, it is displayed in **bold typeface.**

Author's Disclosure

For reasons I do not understand, writers today are supposed to be objective. Few disclose the viewpoints or opinions they use to decide what information is important and what is not, or what shall be presented or omitted.

I do not adhere to this standard and make no pretense of being objective. I am biased in favor of liberty, free markets, and international neutrality and proud of it. So I disclose my viewpoint, which you will find explained in detail in my other books.[1]

For those who have not yet read these publications, I call my viewpoint Juris Naturalism (pronounced *jur*-es *nach*-e-re-liz-em, sometimes abbreviated JN) meaning the belief in a natural law that is higher than any government's law. Here are six quotes from America's Founders that help to describe this viewpoint:

> ...all men are created equal, that they are endowed by their Creator with certain unalienable rights.
> — Declaration of Independence, 1776

> The natural rights of the colonists are these: first, a right to life; second to liberty; third to property; together with the right to support and defend them in the best manner they can.
> — Samuel Adams, 1772

---

[1] See Richard Maybury's other Uncle Eric books (see pgs. 6-13), published by Bluestocking Press, web site: www.BluestockingPress.com

It is strangely absurd to suppose that a million of human beings collected together are not under the same moral laws which bind each of them separately.
— Thomas Jefferson, 1816

A wise and frugal government, which shall restrain men from injuring one another, which shall leave them otherwise free to regulate their own pursuits of industry and improvement, and shall not take from the mouth of labor the bread it has earned. This is the sum of good government.
— Thomas Jefferson, 1801

Not a place on earth might be so happy as America. Her situation is remote from all the wrangling world, and she has nothing to do but to trade with them.
— Thomas Paine, 1776

The great rule of conduct for us, in regard to foreign nations, is, in extending our commercial relations, to have with them as little political connection as possible.
— George Washington, 1796

George
Washington

Part One

How the Mind Works

1

How We Understand Our World

Dear Chris,

Thanks for your letter. I am glad to hear you have been thinking about your future, wondering what plans you should be making. I'll do my best to answer your questions.

You asked how to achieve success in your business, career, and investments. There is no easy answer. Much of what I have to offer you about this is my opinion based on my own experiences, many of these learned from the **school of hard knocks** where I have spent a lot of time; so, let's get started.

I'll begin with a short story.

One day I was watching a pro football game between the San Francisco 49ers and the New York Yankees. In one of the plays, the quarterback stepped up to the 60-yard line, took the snap, swung the bat, hit it over the right field fence, and it swished right through the basket for two points.

Chris, what do you know about what I just wrote?

You know it did not happen.

But you were not there. You did not see it. How do you know it did not happen?

You know because you understand something about how football, baseball, and basketball work. You know the rules. You know what goes together and what does not. You know the likely sequence of events. So, you know it could not have happened the way I said it did.

Even though you were not there, you know I am not telling the truth because you have in your mind **models** of how these games work, and what I was telling you did not fit the football, baseball, and basketball models.

Suppose I said that not long ago I was standing on the beach at the ocean and saw a ship come over the horizon toward me. First I saw the hull, then the masts.

Again, you know I am wrong. You were not there, but you know the information you are receiving is not correct because you know the earth is a sphere.

In your mind's eye you visualize a globe and because you know the earth is round, you know that standing on the beach a person first sees the ship's masts and then the hull as it comes over the horizon.

You were not there, but you know it did not happen the way I said because the model in your mind tells you so.

The data do not fit your model.

That gives you a choice. Either the data are wrong or your model is wrong.

Which do you think it is?

In the case of the football game, when I said the quarterback hit the ball over the right field fence, what was your instant reaction?

Did you think your understanding of football must be wrong? Or did you think Uncle Eric must be wrong?

You doubted me, right? It did not even occur to you to question your model; instead, you questioned the data.

Humans are very reluctant to throw out their models. They will reject data very quickly, but not models. This is because models are so important.

Let me emphasize, Chris, that models are crucial. Models are how humans understand their world.

More about models in my next letter.

Uncle Eric

P.S. Before you read further, I suggest you get a pencil or highlighter, so that as you read these letters you can underline or highlight the points that are important to you. Then, after you have finished all the letters, leaf back through them and reread these points. This will help you remember the things you want to store away for future use.

2

Building Mental Pictures

Dear Chris,

A model is a mental picture of how the world works. Sometimes models are called **paradigms** (pair-a-dimes).

When someone drops an old model and adopts a new one, this is called a **paradigm shift**.

Most of us don't realize it, but we devote a lot of time and effort to testing and improving our models, or paradigms, so we have a lot of faith in them. Models are rugged. They are not infallible, but they are tough.

Chris, I believe one of the most important things we should all learn at a very early age is, *models are how we think, they are the way we understand how the world works.*

As we go through life we build these very complex pictures in our minds of how the world works — and we constantly refer back to them, matching incoming data against our models. That's how we make sense of things.

Chris, suppose you wake up in the middle of the night. You discover you are standing upright and in complete darkness. You realize you have been sleepwalking. You cannot see anything and do not know what room you are in.

You reach out and touch something. The refrigerator. Are you in the living room? The bathroom? You match the incoming data against your mental paradigm of your house and realize you are in the kitchen.

Using data and your model, you know exactly where you stand, so you can now walk through the darkness to the light switch and flip it on.

Everyday we match incoming data against our paradigms to try to make sense of things.

Let me give you another example. Your car will not start. You turn the key and the engine cranks, but it does not start.

If you know something about automobiles — if you have a mental model of how a car works — you instantly realize it must be one of three things. A gasoline engine runs on a mixture of fuel, air, and electricity — the electricity causes the fuel and air to explode. This moves the pistons, which turn the crankshaft and wheels.

If there is no explosion, your model tells you there's probably a shortage of fuel, air, or electricity. You start tracing these three systems to discover which one broke down.

Here is a key point: Without that model of how an engine works, you do not know where to start because you do not know what is important and what is not.

The car will not start, so you check the ashtray. It's full. You empty it, but the car still will not start.

Then you top off the windshield washer fluid. The car still will not start.

If a person does this, you know his model of how a car works is way out of touch with reality and he needs to throw out this unworkable model and get a workable one. He needs a paradigm shift.

Notice your model is transferable. Once you learn the fuel-air-electricity model for a Toyota, then it works as well for a Volkswagen or Ford, as long as all the cars have gasoline engines.

Chris, because models are so important, we give a lot of care and attention to improving them. We are always trying to make them better, and this makes life easier for us. If the car won't start, we do not waste time checking the tire pressure.

Uncle Eric

3

Sorting Data

Dear Chris,

One of the most important uses for models is in sorting incoming information to decide if it is important or not.

For instance, part of your model for how the human body works is: as the human body ages the hair turns gray.

Suppose you are 50 years old and you notice your hair turning gray. Should you see a doctor about it?

Probably not. Your model of the human body tells you this is not unusual; it is nothing to worry about.

Suppose you are 16 and your hair turns gray.

Now you go to a doctor because your model tells you this is important.

In most schools, models are never mentioned because the teachers are unaware of them. Teachers teach what they were taught and no one ever mentioned models to them, so very few schools teach about them.

For the most part, students are just loaded down with collections of facts they are made to memorize.

Without good models, or paradigms, students have no way to know which facts are important and which are not. Teachers have no way to know this either, so most teachers teach what they were taught.

Chris, to illustrate this point, I'll spend a page or two on a subject all Americans are taught, and most probably think they understand rather well — the importance of George Washington.

What is so important about George Washington?
He was the "father of our country."

What does that mean?
He was the first president.

Big deal, so he was first.
Well then, he won the Revolutionary War.

No, he didn't. It may not be an exaggeration to say Washington was a military disaster. If his strategy had been followed consistently throughout the colonies, the war would have been lost. He tried to fight **set-piece battles**[2] against an army that was probably the world's best at set-piece battles.

What worked in the Revolutionary War was **guerrilla**[3] **tactics** like those of the **Minutemen** at the battle of Concord. These tactics were used mostly by independent **militia** units

---

[2] Set-piece battle: Clashes between highly trained, uniformed armies arranged in battle formations with rigid command structures. Contrasted with guerrilla battles, in which command structures are informal or nonexistent, and volunteers in civilian clothing conduct hit-and-run raids, then disappear. Typically, guerrillas have no central authority on which an enemy can concentrate his forces to compel a surrender.

[3] See previous footnote about set-piece battles.

— guerrillas — who had little connection with George Washington.[4]

Perhaps the most famous example of a guerrilla commander was "Swamp Fox" Francis Marion, considered the father of the U.S. Army Special Forces or "Green Berets." Marion's troops rarely numbered more than 200 and often just a few dozen. Using guerrilla tactics, this handful of part-time troops kept thousands of the enemy tied down and prevented the successful occupation of the whole state of South Carolina. This while Washington lost battle after battle and scored outright victories in only three (Trenton, Princeton, and Yorktown).

Chris, in my opinion, Washington is important mostly because of something few of us have ever heard about — the Newburgh Crisis. In 1783, many people wanted a new government, and army officers planned to set up a **dictatorship** and make Washington the **dictator**.

---

[4] CONCEIVED IN LIBERTY by Murray Rothbard, 1979, Arlington House, Vol. IV gives a detailed look at the battles of the American Revolution. A consistent pattern emerges. Washington was trying to fight the war on the enemy's terms, while independent militia operating as guerrillas relied on the "unfair" tactics of stealth and marksmanship. The enemy could beat Washington but not the guerrillas because they could not find the guerrillas.

Washington not only turned the offer down, he said any soldier who followed the orders of this new government was wrong. A soldier's job was to protect **liberty**, not necessarily to obey orders.

Under Washington's encouragement, the troops mutinied and deserted, and this kept America from becoming a dictatorship.[5]

As I see it, nothing else Washington did comes close to the importance of the choice he made in the Newburgh Crisis. He resisted the temptation to be a dictator and, instead, recommended that the troops rebel and opt for the system of liberty.

Chris, how many people do you know who would have the ethics to walk away from the opportunity to be ruler of America?

Few curriculums mention the Newburgh Crisis. Why? I can only speculate.

But the fact remains that if teachers do not teach about the Newburgh Crisis, students will not learn that Washington encouraged his troops to disobey orders — Washington wanted the troops dedicated to a **Higher Law** than any **government's law**.

This is not likely to be a popular idea in **government-controlled schools**.

Incidentally, Chris, this is what the **Nuremberg Trials** were about after World War II. The judges said there is a Higher Law than any government's law, and we must all obey

---

[5] See THE REVOLUTIONARY YEARS, edited by Mortimer J. Adler, published by Encyclopedia Britannica. Out of print. Also, CONCEIVED IN LIBERTY by Murray Rothbard, 1979, Arlington House, Vol. IV, Chapter 72, the Newburgh Conspiracy.

this Higher Law. **Nazi** leaders did not, so they were imprisoned or hanged.

The principle of a Higher Law is not taught in the schools, or at least not in many schools, which is why a great deal of what is taught does not make much sense. There is no model for analyzing geopolitical events. At age eighteen when most students graduate high school, all they remember about George Washington is that he chopped down a cherry tree. (Or did he?) His handling of the Newburgh Crisis — his decision to obey a Higher Law — remains almost completely forgotten, and the Higher Law model unknown.

I will write to you in depth about the Higher Law model in another set of letters I'll title WHATEVER HAPPENED TO JUSTICE? For now, what I want you to know is that without this model of Higher Law, the real importance of Washington is lost.

Chris, let's turn to current events in the city named after George Washington. Here is a paragraph from the book A TIME FOR ACTION, by former U.S. Treasury Secretary William Simon:

> One of the things I learned during my tenure in Washington is that the civics book picture of government in operation is completely inaccurate. The idea that our elected officials take part in a careful decision-making process — monitoring events, reviewing options, responsibly selecting policies — has almost no connection with reality. A more accurate image would be that of a runaway train with the throttle stuck wide open — while the passengers and crew are living it up in the dining car.

Notice this former U.S. Treasury Secretary is telling us that the model of government taught in school is wrong, and he is giving us another model — the runaway train — that his experience tells him is closer to the truth. The former Treasury Secretary is recommending a paradigm shift to a model the government does not want us to have.

So, Chris, models are how humans understand their world. If you want to understand how the world works and how to cope with it successfully, think in terms of learning good models.

Facts are nice, but models are essential. When trying to learn something, start by asking for the model.

Uncle Eric

P.S. Chris, all of my letters on history, **economics**, and **geopolitics** (meaning world politics) are built around the same Higher Law model that George Washington used.

4

Where is the Evidence?

Dear Chris,

We are human, and humans are **fallible,** so no model is 100% accurate. Everything we do is flawed to some extent.

What **standard of proof** do we use to decide if something should be incorporated into our model or not?

Chris, it's a personal choice. It depends on how important the model is to you.

For instance, I have no interest in cooking. Doing laundry, ironing, cleaning — okay, I will do those, but I really hate to cook. I'm afraid if I learn to cook, I will end up doing the cooking, so my standard of proof on how an apple pie is constructed is very low.

If you told me that if I run out of apples I could substitute crackers, I would not question it. I might raise an eyebrow, but that is all because I have no intentions of ever using the apple pie model and no interest in learning it. If I want an apple pie, I go to a bakery where they know the apple pie model and use it well.

On the other hand, I have a very strong interest in earning a high return on my **investments**, so I spend a lot of time and energy learning how the **economy**[6] works. And, I am diligent about applying a rule I wish everyone would teach children. Chris, on things that are important to me, I continually ask, *Where is the evidence? Show me the evidence.*

The investment markets are crammed with sales pitches for why you should buy this investment or that investment. All these pitches include information about the past performance and expected performance of the investment. Usually you will see a line rising on a chart. A slang term for these graphics is **mountain charts**.

A mountain chart is not evidence. It is a line drawn by someone who wants us to believe him. He wants us to see him as an **expert** we can trust.

I do not want to see those lines. I want to see the actual prices at which the investments traded in the markets.

A **price** is not just a statistic; it is an event. It is something that really happened. Buyer and seller came together and made a trade. They agreed on a price. A price is an event, and an event cannot be changed.

When experts draw their lines, they use averages, trends, and projections. None of this is real evidence, it is guesswork extracted from the evidence. It is **opinion**.

For instance, by using averages, the person who draws the line can make the line much smoother than the reality. If you do not know a lot about **statistics**, you can be led to think the investment does not make wild, frightening swings.

I want to see the real evidence. Show me the actual prices that real, live, breathing investors paid. That is evidence because that is reality.

---

[6] Economy: the system for producing and distributing goods and services. The economy is the source of jobs, and of all the human-made things we have.

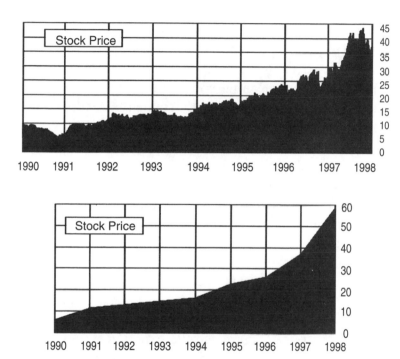

Which of these companies would you rather invest in?

Actually, it is the same company. Both "mountain" charts are 100% accuate, but the data have been selected and displayed differently.

The company is Xerox. The top chart is the *daily* average from 1990 *to* 1998. The bottom is the *yearly* average from 1990 *through* 1998.

Where is the evidence? Show me the evidence.

Chris, you might wonder: How much evidence do you need before you believe something enough to incorporate it into your model of how the world works?

The more important a model is to you, the higher your standard of proof should be.

Physicists, chemists, and biologists — the so-called **"hard" sciences**, meaning solid and reliable — have the easiest time answering this question, much easier than **"soft" sciences** such as economics, psychology, or sociology.

In the hard sciences, the generally accepted standard of proof is reproducibility. It is easy to do experiments on atoms, molecules, and bugs, so numerous experiments can be done to check results. In the "soft" sciences, we cannot experiment on humans, so in these sciences, proof is hard to nail down.

In the 1980s two scientists in Utah said they had discovered a way to get a net gain in energy from cold fusion. Chris, we do not hear much about them any more because no one else could do their experiment and get the same results.

Until others can reproduce the experiment and get the same outcome, the idea is considered unproven. It's not considered wrong, just unproven so far.

And, no one will invest their hard-earned money in building a cold fusion power plant until many people have reproduced the results of the experiment, over and over.

That is a very high standard of proof.

Chris, standards of proof are a personal choice, it is up to you to decide how much evidence is enough. But I hope you have the attitude that in any matter that is highly important to you, you will demand a lot of evidence.

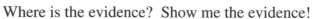

Where is the evidence? Show me the evidence!

This is especially so in regard to matters affecting your money, Chris. Develop the habit of asking, where is the evidence? The world is full of con artists and thieves, as well as persons who are well-meaning but misguided. Many are highly persuasive about where you should put your money. I could tell you horror stories for days.

A polite way to handle the problem is to say: I have an open mind to the possibility that this may pay off, but I am a cautious person and it is my policy to always ask for evidence.

Then question that evidence.

What is the source?

How reliable is this source?

If the source is an expert, what makes this person an expert?

There is an old question that is a bit rude, so you won't want to ask it very often, but keep it in the back of your mind: If you are so smart, why aren't you rich?

Also, Chris, it is not enough to be an expert, it is also necessary to be an unbiased expert. If the person stands to benefit when you follow his or her advice, then demand more evidence. This is not to say he or she is dishonest or that the advice is wrong, but when it comes to your money, never drop your guard until you are absolutely certain it is safe to do so.

It has been my experience that persons who go broke the fastest are generally the ones who have low standards of proof. These are the people who never ask, where is the evidence?

Generally, the ones who are wealthiest are the ones who require the most evidence before they commit their money.

Incidentally, Chris, whenever an expert confronts you, in the interest of protecting yourself, always look for a hidden **agenda**.[7] If this person is trying to persuade you to do something, ask why? Is there anything in it for this person?

Again, this is not to say he or she is crooked, but if someone wants you to do something differently than you otherwise would — if the expert is trying to make you change course — then you should wonder why.

The less evidence you have for committing your money to something, the closer you are to outright gambling. You might as well take your money to a Las Vegas casino.

Summarizing, Chris, the more important the model is to you, the higher should be your standard of proof. Get into the habit of asking, where is the evidence? Show me the evidence.

Uncle Eric

---

[7] Agenda: a list or plan of things to be done.

5

How to Learn or Teach Models

Dear Chris,

I have spent several letters making a case for learning models. Now I'm going to present my case for which models you should learn, and the best way to learn them.

Learning (or teaching) models is easy. Just knowing that this is how our minds work is 90% of the battle because we have an inborn tendency to create models.

For instance, we have all had the experience of trying to teach (or learn) a new board game, such as Monopoly®. If you sit a person down and read all the rules to that person, what happens?

He goes to sleep.

So you say, we'll just play the game for a while and you'll get the idea.

What we are saying is, through experience you will build the model in your mind automatically.

Experience creates models automatically.

Humans build models without knowing they are doing it.

So do animals. Your dog or cat cannot read a floor plan, but he learns the layout of your house so well he can walk through it in the dark, just like you can.

The dog or cat has never heard of models, knows nothing about them, but creates them in his head anyhow. Even at these basic levels, experience creates models automatically.

This is why classroom instruction via lecture is the least effective way to teach, and why hands-on learning-by-doing is the most effective. We are made in such a way that we build models automatically by doing.

Typically, classroom instruction is like teaching a person to play Monopoly® just by making him memorize the rules and then giving him a test on these rules. If he flunks the test, he is made to study the rules more and tested again.

Chris, how long do you think the Monopoly® rules would be remembered if that is how the player learned them?

Unfortunately, some models are impossible to learn using a hands-on process, so one method humans use to substitute for real world experience is telling stories. Stories are used to demonstrate and illustrate ideas.

If you are having difficulty learning a model (or anything else) ask the teacher to give you an example by telling a story. If the story is well told, your mind will translate it into a model automatically.

For example, would you like to hear a story?

I believe you are familiar with the story of the boy who cried wolf. A young shepherd is told to watch the sheep. If the young shepherd sees a wolf, he is to cry "Wolf!" "Wolf!" and help will come immediately. He finds it greatly entertaining to cry "Wolf!" when there is no wolf. Groups of rescuers quickly hurry to his aid; to the young shepherd it is a wonderful joke. Then one day a wolf appears. He cries "Wolf!" and no one comes; the young shepherd is eaten.

This model is taught in the form of a story rather than a carefully formulated rule because a story is much easier for a young child to grasp.

Suppose that, instead of hearing the story, children are made to memorize the model it teaches: "Truthfulness protects credibility. Never sound a warning in the absence of a real threat. False warnings reduce credibility and ruin your odds of receiving help when you really need it."

How many children would remember that? I don't really know, but I'm reasonably certain that considerably more will remember the model because of the story rather than the model without the story.

Chris, stories that include concrete examples create models automatically.

Uncle Eric

6

Two Highly Important Models

Dear Chris,

The two models with which I am most familiar and that I think are crucially important for everyone to learn are **Austrian economics** and the old **British common law**. Chris, since you want this current set of letters to provide you with an overview of what you need for success in your career, business, and investments, I will only briefly discuss Austrian economics and British common law at this time. However, I plan to write you in depth about these subjects in future sets of letters[8] (I'll call them WHATEVER HAPPENED TO PENNY CANDY? and WHATEVER HAPPENED TO JUSTICE?) and I think that when you read these letters you will realize why I believe that these models are so important.

---

[8] Uncle Eric is referring to Richard J. Maybury's books WHATEVER HAPPENED TO PENNY CANDY? and WHATEVER HAPPENED TO JUSTICE? published by Bluestocking Press, web site: www.BluestockingPress.com. WHATEVER HAPPENED TO PENNY CANDY? is a short course in economics for people who hate economics. WHATEVER HAPPENED TO JUSTICE? is a short course in the history of law, and it shows the connection between rational law and economic progress.

I will do my best to make these letters about economics very clear and fun to read. They will be based on the so-called Austrian view of economics — "Austrian" because the founders were from Austria.

My letters about the old British common law will be a short course in the history of law, and will show the connection between rational law and economic progress.

These sets of letters on economics and law will provide an overall model of how human civilization works, especially in regard to how we become financially prosperous, both as a group and as individuals. The letters will provide a foundation for the specific nuts-and-bolts tactics you can use in your everyday life.

Chris, Austrian economics is the economic model that I believe is backed by the most persuasive evidence. For instance, two books written in the 1940s, ROAD TO SERFDOM by F.A. Hayek and PLANNED CHAOS by Ludwig von Mises, had amazing foresight and both were based on Austrian economics.

Austrian economics is the most free-market of all economic models, and it is the one that is most in agreement with the ethical principles on which America was founded. (Chris, these ethical principles will be explained in depth in WHATEVER HAPPENED TO JUSTICE?)

Austrian economics sees the economy not as a machine (as other economic models do) but as an **ecology** made of biological organisms — humans. The top two Austrian economists were Ludwig von Mises and his student F.A. Hayek. Hayek won a Nobel Prize. I recommend that you read anything written by Mises or Hayek.

The principles on which America was founded were those of the old British common law.

Underlying the common law are two basic rules. These rules are the point at which all religions intersect, the point on which all agree. Common to all religions, these laws were the foundation of the old common law. These two laws are: 1) do all you have agreed to do, and 2) do not encroach on other persons or their property.

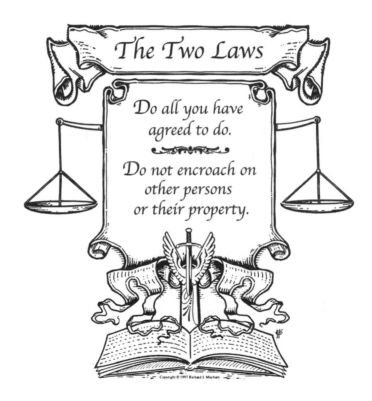

If this sounds at all complicated, Chris, don't worry. As the saying goes, "It will all become perfectly clear" by the time you finish reading my sets of letters on economics and law.

My main point now is that, in my opinion, you and your family and friends will avoid a lot of trouble, and find success of every kind much easier to achieve, if you adopt these two models, Austrian economics and common law.

However, they are not taught by many schools, so they must be self-taught or taught by parents who have already learned the model. Otherwise, individuals will probably be forced to stumble through life without them. This is why I plan to write you the sets of letters on economics and law. After you finish reading them I encourage you to share them with everyone you care about.

Uncle Eric

7

History Without Models

Dear Chris,

One of the most dangerous weaknesses in traditional education is that it contains no model for political history. Children are taught unconnected collections of facts — the Battle of Hastings was fought in 1066, John Adams was America's second president, the Allies won the world wars — without any way to tie it together and make sense of it.

The student leaves school thinking history is a waste of time, a collection of **trivia.** Then, deprived of the real lessons history has to offer, he or she is vulnerable and gets tangled up in disasters such as the Vietnam War, as I did when I was young.

Chris, try this. When studying or teaching history, see it not in terms of rich vs. poor, or man vs. nature — both of which are popular models in today's news media and entertainment industry — but in terms of Higher Law vs. political power. I think you will find history makes a lot more sense and it will be much more useful in understanding and coping with the forces that affect your everyday life.

Incidentally, Chris, in WHATEVER HAPPENED TO JUSTICE? I plan to include a suggested parent-child agreement.[9] If you use this agreement, you and your family will be living common law principles in your everyday lives and, by doing so, developing a much better understanding of the law. You will build your models automatically. I will also include a teacher-student agreement for classroom use.

Three good sources for materials that agree with Austrian economics and common law are:

Bluestocking Press
PO Box 1014 • Dept. TA2
Placerville, CA 95667-1014
(800) 959-8586
www.BluestockingPress.com

Foundation for Economic Education
30 S. Broadway
Irvington-on-Hudson, NY 10533.
(800) 960-4FEE
www.fee.org

Laissez Faire Books
7123 Interstate 30, Suite 42
Little Rock, AR 72209
800-326-0996
www.lfb.com

---

[9] Uncle Eric is referring to Richard J. Maybury's book WHATEVER HAPPENED TO JUSTICE? The agreement between parent and child, as well as an agreement between teacher and student, are included in the back matter of this book published by Bluestocking Press, web site: www.BluestockingPress.com.

Chris, you might also want to get the fine audio series on economics produced by Knowledge Products. At the time I write this, these are also available from Bluestocking Press.

Knowledge Products
PO Box 305151
Nashville, TN 37230

Another good way to teach the principles of common law is to post a copy of the two fundamental laws (Do all you have agreed to do, and do not encroach on other persons or their property.) on your refrigerator. As I mentioned, I will be explaining these laws, and common law, in more detail in WHATEVER HAPPENED TO JUSTICE?

Meanwhile, refer to them each time there is a dispute or other problem in your family. (These will also be helpful in helping you analyze issues at school, in society, or your workplace.)

You will find this a big help in resolving problems, and you will evolve your own family's case law, so you will be living and breathing real common law. This is not only a way to learn, it is a way to lubricate the machinery of your family's everyday life.

Chris, to help you locate books and authors who are generally in agreement with the Austrian economic model and the common law legal model, I will provide you with a set of guidelines that are consistent with the principles of America's Founders that I will call EVALUATING BOOKS — WHAT WOULD THOMAS JEFFERSON THINK ABOUT THIS?[10]

---

[10] Uncle Eric is referring to Richard J. Maybury's book EVALUATING BOOKS — WHAT WOULD THOMAS JEFFERSON THINK ABOUT THIS? published by Bluestocking Press, web site: www.BluestockingPress.com

Actually, the guidelines can also be applied to films, media commentators, current events, the Internet — to any written or spoken medium. By applying these guidelines, you will help build and reinforce your models.

Remember, Chris, experience creates models automatically. You and your family *will* build models whether you intend to or not, so be selective.

Uncle Eric

8

A Model for Selecting Models

Dear Chris,

Earlier I said, "All day long every day we match incoming data against our models to try to make sense of things."

What if we don't have a model for a particular piece of data?

We search for an existing model — or start building one ourselves.

How do we know we have a good model?

There are lots of models for selecting models. One is to flip a coin. Do you believe in the geocentric model of the solar system, or the heliocentric model? (Geocentric means the belief that the earth is the center of the solar system. Heliocentric means the sun is the center.)

Heads, geocentric; tails, heliocentric.

Experience shows the coin-flip model tends to be right only 50% of the time, so, if you want a higher percentage of accuracy, you need to find other models for selecting models.

We can ask the advice of persons who have prestige. For instance, we can ask a famous baseball player, heliocentric or geocentric?

It might work, but asking someone who is a prestigious specialist in the field that concerns us, astronomy, would probably yield better results.

However, there are problems with the prestige model. For one, most specialists spend their lives working with widely accepted models. If an accepted model is wrong, the specialists have so much time, energy, and ego invested in it that they may be reluctant to give it up.

The classic case — one of the most important incidents in world history — is that of astronomer Galileo.

Studying the heavens through the newly invented telescope, Galileo discovered Copernicus[11] was right. The earth is not the center of the solar system, the sun is. In 1632, Galileo published his findings.

Galileo's evidence and conclusions were thought by many to contradict the Bible. These people believed the Bible teaches a model in which the earth is the center of all God's creation. (Chris, please note, when talking about the earth or sun as the center of the solar system, I am talking about measurable, physical facts, not religious beliefs about man being the center of God's attention.)

In other words, the prestigious experts of Galileo's day were wedded to a model, that of the geocentric solar system, which was scientifically false. Instead of keeping an open mind about Galileo's data, they chose to muzzle and punish him. Today we honor Galileo, and we regard those experts as closed-minded tyrants. People who choose to rely on the words of prestigious experts are reminded, remember Galileo.

---

[11] Copernicus believed that the planets revolved around the sun and that the turning of the earth on its axis accounted for the apparent rising and setting of the sun and stars.

Another problem with the prestige model is that even people who are honorable, highly intelligent, and open-minded are still human, and humans make mistakes — honest mistakes, but mistakes nevertheless.

A third model for selecting models is to do our own research. Start from scratch gathering data until your mind forms a model. This can work, but it can also be enormously time consuming and labor intensive, and in the end you still do not know if your mind formed a model that truly describes reality. The astronomers who said Galileo was wrong based their argument not only on passages in the Bible but on the mountains of data that had been collected by thousands of astronomers since the beginning of history. Their reaction to Galileo was, you are only one man and you have been working with this newfangled telescope gadget only five years; how can you be so arrogant as to question the wisdom of history's most brilliant thinkers, including Aristotle and Ptolemy[12]?

Chris, if you had been an astronomer back then, what would have been your reaction to Galileo's claims? Would you have had the courage to agree that Aristotle and Ptolemy were wrong?

Here is another angle to the problem of believing you know what is correct.

There is a mathematical reason why, if everyone believes something, this can be strong evidence everyone is wrong.

The human technological world and the natural world are both unimaginably complex. No one can know very much about many things, so we have become a civilization of specialists. We do not go to the same person to have our

---

[12] Ptolemy. Astronomer who supposed the earth to be the center of the universe and the sun and stars to revolve around it.

appendix removed and our carburetor adjusted. We go to specialists — a doctor and a mechanic.

The only knowledge everyone, or even just the majority, can be right about is knowledge that is very simple. Is it raining? What time is it? Who won the Superbowl?

Beyond such simple questions, too much data is available and too much knowledge is needed for everyone to have a deep understanding of everything. So, if a majority has looked at any given complex subject and developed an opinion about it, then odds are very high that the majority is wrong. Fifty-one percent of the population cannot be specialists equipped to comprehend a complicated issue.

I do not mean to say the majority is always wrong, Chris. I'm saying only that it is a mathematical fact that the only way for the majority to be right about a complex subject is through luck.

So, Chris, what model do we use to select models? Hundreds of years of experience have yielded this six-step procedure:

1. Gather evidence.
2. Examine the evidence.
3. Hypothesize (make an educated guess) about its meaning.
4. Test the hypothesis.
5. If the test yields the expected results, invite a large number of others to duplicate the test to see if they get the same results.
6. If all get the same results, accept the hypothesis as fact; or, at least call it a "**working hypothesis**," meaning it will be taken as fact until it is proven wrong.

Chris, this is called the **scientific method**.

It's not perfect.

But it is the best way I know to make discoveries in which we can have a great deal of confidence.

Not total confidence, but a great deal.

A scientist once pointed out to me that scientific "facts" have so often been found wrong upon investigation with newer models and equipment that many scientists today do not speak of scientific fact at all. They think only in terms of working hypotheses — ideas that are useful and probably right, but also possibly incomplete or wrong.

The only facts these scientists take as 100% reliable are those that have been disproven. For instance, all scientists believe it is an unwavering carved-in-granite fact that the geocentric model of the solar system is wrong.

Chris, this is a good place to point out that for me personally, there are no facts, just working hypotheses. To me, life is very much a choice between open-mindedness and certainty, and I have been stung by certainty so many times that I now prefer always to err on the side of open-mindedness. I always cling to at least a tiny bit of doubt about everything. This is not to say I think everything is false. It is to say I admit I will never be intelligent enough to have a complete picture of anything, my view will always be a bit off because I'm not perfect. Indeed, because I am not perfect, certainty is a trap.

More about the scientific method in my next letter.

Uncle Eric

9

Does it Predict?

Dear Chris,

The key to the scientific method is the ability to predict. Does the hypothesis predict the results? And, does it do this every time?

For instance, *before* you drop a bowling ball off the top of a skyscraper, can you predict the exact instant it will hit the ground?

Another way of asking this is, do you have a mathematical formula that exactly describes the speed at which an object falls?

After thousands of people have made the prediction, conducted the test, and seen the prediction come true, then you can have a lot of confidence in your formula.

You will have a way to describe how a small part of the universe works.

If it is true that "by their works ye shall know them," then by learning about this tiny bit of the universe, you have learned a tiny bit about the Creator that made it.

And, you will have a model, or working hypothesis, on which you can rely.

Again, this does not mean we should ever be 100% certain any model is correct — always keep an open mind — but we can have a lot of faith in it.

How much faith?

Every one of the hundreds of thousands of pieces in a Boeing 747 is made according to mathematical models. When we board a 747, we trust our lives to these models.

The same for every piece of an automobile; we trust our lives to these models.

And, we trust our lives to the models used by dentists, electricians, architects, and thousands of others.

This is what the scientific method has done for us. It has delivered the goods, and it has done this with a reliability that is breathtaking.

Would you trust your life to the flip of a coin?

Would you trust your life to the word of a person who happens to be famous?

Would you trust it to the opinion of the majority?

Would you trust it to the scientific method? Whether you realize it or not, you choose to do so every day.

Again, Chris, this does not mean the scientific method is perfect. Maybe in the future someone will come up with something better. But for now, our best model for choosing models is the scientific method.

Remember, Chris, the scientific method's most important feature is the question, can this model make successful predictions?

Uncle Eric

P.S. Chris, Galileo's case was one of the first to cause people to believe science and religion are enemies. Some still believe it.

My personal view is that there is no need for conflict. Science and religion are two different realms of thought. Religion, or, if you prefer, philosophy, picks up where science leaves off. Or perhaps another way to say it is, religion leads and science follows. Religion generates endless questions — this is one of its main purposes, to make us think — and science is one of the tools we can use to answer some of those questions.

I recently met a scientist, anthropologist Hank Wesselman, who used the scientific method to investigate scores of religions around the world. Author of the book SPIRITWALKER, Dr. Wesselman has come to believe even highly diverse religions have things in common. The most important, says Wesselman, is that religions have discovered a spiritual world that is not readily apparent to those who live in a highly technological society. Technology is not necessarily bad, but it tends to block vision.

I am not sure I agree with all of Wesselman's work, but it does make me curious about what science and religion will discover about each other in the future.

10

A Way to Test a Model
You Are Not Qualified to Test

Dear Chris,

Even though you may not know much about a given model, you can sometimes test its accuracy by checking it against models you do understand.

For instance, suppose you know a lot about chemistry but little about medicine. You have a medical problem, athlete's foot, so you consult a medical expert. The expert tells you that you can cure athlete's foot by drinking one-tenth of an ounce of water. Knowing about chemistry, you know one-tenth of an ounce of water is such a tiny percentage of the water in the body that it is unlikely to have a noticeable effect on anything, so this would instantly tell you that the model this "expert" is using is no good. His model deals with medicine, not chemistry, but you know it is wrong because you know its use of chemistry is wrong.

In other words, Chris, if you are not an expert in the field a model deals with, try to test that model against what you do know.

If I know about football but not baseball and someone tells me the quarterback kicked the ball deep into right field, then I can be confident this person knows as little about baseball as I do.

Uncle Eric

11

Beware of Tautology

Dear Chris,

When judging the accuracy of a model, beware of **tautologies**.

According to the AMERICAN HERITAGE DICTIONARY, a tautology (pronounced taught-ology) is "an empty or vacuous statement composed of simpler statements in a fashion that makes it logically true whether the simpler statements are factually true or false."

In other words, tautologies are always logically true but they are also worthless.

An example would be the statement, either the sun will come out or it won't. This statement is true, but what does it really tell us?

Tautologies are not necessarily bad, but they can be highly deceptive.

An example of a harmless tautology is the statement: Too much sugar is bad for you.

"Too much" means the same as "bad," so the statement cannot be false; it is the same as saying, bad is bad.

Another example of a harmless tautology: the survivors are alive.

Well, of course they are alive, the definition of survivor is a person who managed to stay alive.

Harmful tautologies are often not so easily spotted because many are designed to deceive. To illustrate, I've made up the following example:

Adolph Hitler is a wise and honorable man who is deeply concerned about building a better world for us all. We find his plan in his book MEIN KAMPF, which explains what is wrong with the world and how to fix it. We know MEIN KAMPF is profoundly true because this wise and honorable man wrote it. And we know he is wise and honorable because only such a man could write the profound truths in this book.

We can call this the "Hitler is our savior" model. Notice that the presentation does not go outside Hitler and his book. There is no independent evidence. Hitler is good because his book proves it, and we know his book is right because Hitler wrote it.

Circular reasoning.

Chris, you might think this example is silly, who could possibly fall for it? But millions did.

The world is full of tautological models. One of the best examples is this:

The majority is always correct.
How do we know?
Because the definition of correct is: what the majority has voted for.

Circular reasoning. It is hard to believe people fall for this, but millions have. It is the basis of the U.S. legal system today, which has mutated from the legal principles on which America was founded.

Today, the premise of all laws in the U.S. is majority rule. I will explain more about this in my set of letters on law (WHATEVER HAPPENED TO JUSTICE?).

Talking with a fellow teacher about 30 years ago, I asked him how he planned to vote in the upcoming elections. In all seriousness, he answered that he wanted to do the right thing, so he would wait to see the direction the majority was headed and he would vote that way.

Within the context of the U.S. legal system, the teacher's logic made perfect sense.

It was not always so. The American Founders did not plan a tautological legal system, but that is what the system has mutated into, as you will see when you read WHATEVER HAPPENED TO JUSTICE?

So, Chris, before you adopt a model, always ask, is it tautological? One good way to check this is to ask: Is this model built on circular reasoning, or is it supported by evidence that is independent of the model?

If there is no outside verification, the model might still be correct, but it is also likely to be worthless.

Yes, too much sugar is bad for you, but what does this really tell us?

Uncle Eric

12

How to Control People

Dear Chris,

The world is full of people who like to play God. They have a plan and they want us to follow it.

Their problem is that controlling a person against his will is difficult. If you have ever visited a maximum-security prison, you have some idea of how much money, time, and labor is invested in cells, fences, barbed wire, weapons, and other resources to control those who do not want to be controlled.

Even then, forcible control does not work very well. Despite these extremely tight security conditions, prisoners commonly get their hands on weapons, drugs, and other contraband.[13] Sometimes they escape or riot.

How is a **powerseeker** to keep control of an entire country's population?

The easiest way is for the powerseeker to convince the people they should behave according to the powerseeker's agenda.

---

[13] Contraband: illegal goods.

The surest way to do this is to insert in people's minds models that serve the agenda.

At one time this could be done easily by controlling the facts people received. The human mind creates models automatically, so if you control the facts the mind sees, you control the model the mind creates. The person then behaves according to the model. He or she is your own personal robot and probably does not realize it.

This is why the American Founders were so intent on protecting freedom of speech, freedom of the press, and freedom of religion. They did not want anyone controlling the flow of information because they knew controlled data leads to controlled models, which yields controlled behavior.

Today, however, after the invention of the printing press, radio, telephone, TV, and the Internet, controlling facts has become almost impossible. A short cut — direct insertion of the model — has become essential if a powerseeker wants to control a population.

This is why all tyrants try to keep an iron grip on their school systems. When a government controls the schools, it does not need to control the press; it already has control of the people's models. Without realizing it, the people automatically ignore information the tyrant wants them to ignore because models inserted into their minds when they were children tell them this information is unimportant.

I have read a considerable amount of history, Chris, and I have noticed a pattern among tyrants. When they come to power, they first seize people's guns, then news organizations, and then schools. Schools seem to be the most important prize because once a tyrant controls schools, he does not need to control much else because he controls the models.

Uncle Eric

P.S. Chris, to some extent, whenever you accept someone else's model you accept (perhaps unknowingly) this person's agenda.

For instance, we cannot be sure what was really in the minds of Copernicus and Galileo, but very likely these astronomers were in search of scientific truth. So, when you accept their heliocentric model, you are accepting their quest for scientific truth. And, you are choosing this truth over the beliefs of highly respected experts of that era.

A person who accepts the socialist central planning economic model of Lenin and Stalin accepts Lenin's and Stalin's belief that government "experts" have the right and duty to plan each person's life and to punish anyone who does not follow the plan, even if the plan is harmful. (You will learn more about this in other sets of my letters.)

The same goes for the ideas I am trying to teach you. I have agendas, too. Everyone does, this is part of life. Let me explain mine clearly.

I am a great admirer of Patrick Henry, James Madison, and the other American Founders (as well as scientists such as Copernicus and Galileo). I believe many of the problems of our world today are due to our drift away from the system of liberty the Founders tried to begin. I want very much to return to this system of liberty and to see it develop and flower. The model my letters teach has this as one of its goals. So, be aware, Chris, that after you finish my letters, if you decide to accept my model, you will have also accepted my agenda.

And, again, to some extent, whenever you accept anyone's model, you have also, consciously or unconsciously, accepted that person's agenda. Stay aware of this.

13

Cognitive Dissonance

Dear Chris,

This will be one of my most important letters.

If you control people's models, most of the people simply will not see facts that disagree with their models. This is not because they are stupid, it is because of something called **cognitive dissonance**.

Cognitive dissonance happens when a person encounters a fact or persuasive idea that disagrees with his model.

As an example, I will return to the flat earth model. Suppose a person has been raised to believe the earth is flat like a disk, not spherical.

One day he is standing on the shore as a sailing ship comes toward him. First the masts are visible, then the hull.

If the earth were a disk, both the hull and masts would appear at the same time. They would grow in size, from a pinpoint to a complete, detailed image as the ship comes nearer.

But the earth is a sphere, so, first the person sees the masts, then the hull.

If he has lived with the disk model all his life, he may not take notice of the contradiction, or he may dismiss it as an unimportant puzzle that does not require his attention.

If someone calls his attention to the contradiction, he may try to change the subject. If the person persists, he may grow angry, or he may walk away.

Resistance to provable facts that disagree with one's model is cognitive dissonance. Cognitive refers to thinking, and dissonance means disharmony or disagreement.

A key point: cognitive dissonance can cause a reaction that is physiological. If the person is prevented from dismissing the contradiction, he may experience higher blood pressure, nervousness, irritability, and maybe perspiration. Stress.

It is much like hunger or thirst. When a person experiences a severe need for food or water, he will be physically uncomfortable until the need is satisfied; then he will be more relaxed.

The more strongly a fact or persuasive idea counters one's model, the more physical discomfort — tension — one will feel, and the greater will be his desire to ignore the fact or idea, so that he can relax.

Also, the more deeply the model has been ingrained, the more stress the contradiction will cause, and the harder the person will work to ignore it.

This is why those who want to control other people try to impose their models on children as early as possible. The earlier and deeper the model is embedded, the more likely the child, and later the adult, will blindly follow the agenda the model produces.

In 1936, the Hitler Youth Law made membership in the Hitler Youth program mandatory for children age ten and older. After World War II, in Soviet-controlled East Germany, children entered the Young Pioneers at age six.

Cognitive dissonance is the powerseeker's friend, his secret weapon. It is the castle wall protecting the model that causes his victims to follow his agenda.

Cognitive dissonance can be so powerful that if you have a fact or idea that disagrees with a person's model, you should be gentle and polite when you present it to that person. You are likely to cause some pain, perhaps even physical pain; so be careful. I have met people who are so wedded to their models that when they encounter something that challenges them they become violent. This, incidentally, was one of the causes of religious wars during the Middle Ages.[14]

This is also where we get the ancient custom of "shooting the messenger." Sometimes when people receive bad news, they become so emotional they punish the person who delivered the news. In the case of news that undermines a model, the violence can be extreme.

This brings us back to astronomer Galileo.

We all know today that the heliocentric model is correct, but being right can sometimes be hazardous to one's health. Galileo's books were banned. He was arrested, tried, convicted of heresy, sentenced to life in prison, and forced to say his beliefs were wrong.

Philosopher Giordano Bruno also said the geocentric model of the solar system was wrong. In 1592 he was imprisoned for heresy, then in 1600, burned at the stake. That is how much violence cognitive dissonance can sometimes produce.

So, watch for cognitive dissonance, and when you see you are causing it, tread lightly.

---

[14] The Middle Ages were roughly the period 500 AD to 1500 AD.

How can you avoid feeling the pain of cognitive dissonance yourself?

Make part of your model the belief that you are not perfect, you make mistakes. Your models will never be complete, and some might be very wrong.

Anyone's models might be wrong. No human is infallible.

Chris, if you sincerely use phrases such as, "I am rarely certain of anything," or, "my view is just my opinion, it might be wrong," this will not only give you more tolerance of others, and therefore more friends, it will help keep you from experiencing the stress of cognitive dissonance.

It is also a sign of maturity.

So, Chris, it has been my experience that the best protection against cognitive dissonance is open mindedness, or, if you prefer, broad-mindedness. This does not mean you must believe everything you hear, but never dismiss anything out of hand. Always listen thoughtfully and politely to the case the other person tries to make. After all, you want him to do that for you, right?

Uncle Eric

P.S. One of the most important examples of controlling people by controlling their models was the **janissaries** (jan-iss-air-ease). Created during the Middle Ages, the janissaries were soldiers fiercely loyal to the rulers of Turkey. These soldiers were taken from their parents in childhood, then educated and trained to serve the rulers.

Janissaries were even converted to the rulers' religion and forbidden to marry. They lived together in their own barracks and were given special privileges and prestige for their loyalty, which was totally reliable because janissaries had been raised to think the way the rulers wanted them to think.

The effectiveness of the janissary system was so great that the word janissary has been adopted in the English language to mean a highly trained, blindly loyal soldier who does anything he is told, even if it is grossly unethical, and who never questions orders — a human military robot. One goal of the Hitler Youth and Young Pioneers was to create janissaries.

14

How To Stop Learning

Dear Chris,

One of the most important insights about models that I ever learned is this: certainty stops inquiry. It was taught to me by one of my college professors.

The professor pointed out that once we think we have the answer to a question, we stop investigating it. We stop learning.

Before the scientific age, certainty was often deadly. One example: the cause for disease. No one knew that germs caused smallpox, colds, influenza, and other illnesses. Without microscopes, they had no way to detect germs. Many jumped to the conclusion that disease was caused by evil spirits. Because they thought they had the final answer to the question — evil spirits — they did not investigate further. It took many centuries to learn that simple precautions such as washing one's hands before meals could prevent disease and death.

Indeed, if you had a time machine and traveled back to the Middle Ages in Europe where you suggested that washing one's hands would help prevent disease, people would laugh you right back to the present.

Worse, if they tried cleanliness and found it worked, they might have accused you of being a witch and burned you at the stake.

Cognitive dissonance. Shoot the messenger.

Recently, a chemist told me an example of how certainty could have stopped inquiry if a scientist had not followed the scientific method, asking others to check his work. The chemist knew a physicist who was investigating the energy emitted by a radioactive substance.

In his laboratory, the physicist had very sophisticated electronic equipment. This equipment told the physicist that the energy emissions from this substance varied randomly.

Unable to believe the fluctuations, the physicist ran test after test. Finally he was convinced, the emissions did indeed vary randomly. He published his results.

Other physicists were surprised, and tried to duplicate the experiments. None got the same results. In not one of their experiments did the emissions fluctuate.

Several wondered if, in their experiments, they were accidentally doing something different than the first physicist. They asked permission to observe him perform his experiment in his laboratory.

All found they were doing exactly what the first physicist was doing, but in his lab they observed the fluctuations.

Was it his equipment? They tested it, and found it was in good working order.

Eventually the mystery was solved. An elevator down the hall used the same electrical circuit used by the physicist's laboratory. When the elevator was in operation, this caused a slight drop in voltage, which starved the physicist's equipment and caused it to give erroneous readings.

In other words, the embarrassed physicist had not been observing the behavior of energy emitted by a radioactive substance, he had been observing how voltage fluctuations affected his experiment.

Chris, suppose that when he came up with his first measurements, the physicist had decided they were the final answer and he did not need to inquire further. And, suppose the physicist had been so prestigious that other physicists had accepted his measurements as the final answer, and declined to check them.

Certainty stops inquiry. If the physicist's original findings had not been checked and challenged, today's textbooks and college professors would teach the physicist's "discovery" as if it were true, and science students all over the world would incorporate this discovery into their models. Some would try to apply it in their jobs, getting poor results, and wasting untold amounts of time and money.

In short, certainty can be expensive and dangerous.

Another example: before the age of science, many cultures had a tendency to attribute every mystery to a god or gods of one sort or another. If it rained, the rain god had decided to give us wet weather. If it didn't rain, the rain god had decided to give us drought. Whatever the weather, the rain god was the cause.

If we still accepted such all-encompassing explanations as final, we would never have investigated the behavior of ocean currents, winds, and solar radiation, and would never have developed the ability to predict hurricanes. Having no way to know storms were coming, we would not be able to prepare for them, and thousands would die.

So, Chris, beware of certainty. Our models should be always under construction, never finished, and always open to question because we are human, and humans make mistakes.

Uncle Eric

15

Automatic Evil

Dear Chris,

I said earlier that humans are very reluctant to throw out their models. They will throw out data very quickly, but not models.

Once they have been taught a model, even a false one, many will throw out tons of data before they begin to question their model. Cognitive dissonance.

The inability to make a paradigm shift can be especially serious when ethics enter into the subject of models.

If your model is corrupt, it will produce corrupt results automatically without you realizing it. And it will do so in a mass-production fashion, like a factory rolling cars off an assembly line.

I am sure Genghis Kahn[15] thought he was doing an excellent job. Hitler[16] and Stalin,[17] too. Horrible models lead to horrible behavior.

---

[15] Genghis Kahn (c1162-1227): leader of the Mongol Empire. Responsible for the murder and enslavement of millions.

[16] Adolph Hitler (1889-1945): leader of the German Nazi Party. Responsible for the murder and enslavement of millions.

[17] Joseph Stalin (1879-1953): leader of the Union of Soviet Socialist Republics. Responsible for the murder and enslavement of millions.

When you see good people being harmed, question the underlying model.

One model that is, in my opinion, extremely corrupt but very common and widely accepted is the limited liability corporation.

Businesses come in four basic models: **sole proprietorships, partnerships, joint stock companies**, and **limited liability corporations (LLC)**.

Only one person owns a sole proprietorship. This person receives all the profits and bears all the responsibility. If something goes wrong, the proprietor carries the entire burden.

A partnership is the same as a sole proprietorship, except that more than one person owns it. These people share the profits and the responsibilities.

A joint stock company is like a very large partnership. Each owner has shares of stock (certificates of ownership) in the company, and like a partner, is fully responsible for whatever might go wrong.

A limited liability corporation is very different. Like joint stock companies, thousands or millions can own an LLC. But unlike a joint stock company, each owner is responsible only for the amount of his investment, and he can lose only that amount.

This is what **limited liability** means. The investor's risk is limited to the amount of his investment.

Suppose, for instance, 99 people and I each own one share of stock in a limited liability corporation. Also suppose each stockholder's share is worth $100, which means the corporation as a whole is worth $10,000. If the corporation does a million dollars worth of damage to you — if, say, it sells you a faulty product that injures you, causing a million dollars worth of medical bills and lost wages — then by law each of us stockholders loses only our $100, and you get only $10,000. (I am assuming this is a small corporation with no liability insurance.)

So, by law, limited liability corporations are much safer for their owners. If you invest in a proprietorship, partnership, or joint stock company, you are fully liable for any harm your firm might do. Invest in a corporation and your risk is limited to the amount of your investment.

By this artificial legal privilege, corporations are able to attract far more investors than they otherwise would. This deprives proprietorships, partnerships, and joint stock companies of the investment money. (There is only so much money; if you invest one of your dollars in one place that same dollar cannot also be invested in another.) So, limited liability corporations grow at the expense of the other three types of firms.

Limited liability helps grow the giant, highly wasteful corporate bureaucracies depicted in the popular Dilbert™ cartoons.

It also distorts stock markets. Stocks should be the most carefully traded investments because they are the most complex. Instead, shielded by the limited liability privilege, stock markets have become gambling casinos. Millions of people who haven't the foggiest idea how to evaluate a company engage in get-rich-quick speculations.

Owners of limited liability corporations would be a lot more careful if they were fully liable for every mistake their companies made.

We have lived with limited liability corporations for so long that few ever question this model. Limited liability has become a fully accepted part of the economy.

A large part of the entire world economy is run by limited liability corporations, and as the old saying goes, we cannot make a silk purse out of a sow's ear. Unless you plan to be a self-sufficient hermit living in the wilderness, you are stuck in a world built on this model, so your best-laid plans will often go wrong. Get used to it. We cannot extract honesty and safety from something that is, in my opinion, inherently corrupt and deceptive.

Chris, for the rest of your life, the word "scandal" and the word "corporation" will often appear in the same sentence because most owners of large corporations rarely keep a close eye on what their companies are doing. Horrible models lead to horrible behavior.

Uncle Eric

P.S. I am not saying corporations are evil, I'm saying limited liability is evil. Corporations are organizations of people — teams — that accomplish wonders, and they are an important part of the economic system called **capitalism**. For a good explanation of capitalism, see the book CAPITALISM FOR KIDS[18] by Karl Hess published by Bluestocking Press.

---

[18] CAPITALISM FOR KIDS by Karl Hess, published by Bluestocking Press, web site: www.BluestockingPress.com; Phone: 800-959-8586.

16

Models Tend to Merge

Dear Chris,

Year after year, we fine-tune our models of how the world works. Ever so slowly, contradictions disappear and our models come together. Over time, as individuals and as a species, we tend to merge our many small models into a single large one.

For instance, when you were a small child, Chris, your internal map of your world was mostly your home and neighborhood, and, since your grandmother lived close by, the home and neighborhood of your grandmother. As far as geography was concerned, you had only these two very small models. The rest of the world did not exist for you; it was a huge blank space. Even the route between your home and your grandmother's was a blank.

As you grew older, you learned this route, linking and growing your two internal maps into a single larger one. But most of the earth still did not exist for you. Your world was a corridor with your home at one end and your grandmother's at the other.

The years went by and you watched TV. Eventually you learned that there were foreign cities such as Paris and Tokyo.

You knew a little about what these cities looked like, but had no idea where they were or how to travel to them. They were vague spots, tiny models, hanging in space somewhere outside your corridor.

Today you have studied geography and have flown on airliners. You know the location of your home in relation to the rest of the globe and how to travel to far off places.

Your mental map of the earth is not complete in every detail, but it has been fully formed. Your collection of small geographic models has been welded together into this single large one.

Another example. In the 1700s, astronomy, physics, and chemistry were three separate, distinct sciences. Astronomy was rather well developed, and physics was coming along, but chemistry had not advanced much beyond its ancient and misguided predecessor, **alchemy**.

Today the three sciences are so well developed they have merged into what is really a single science. We still make distinctions among them, but the dividing lines are fuzzy. Where does chemistry end and physics begin? Where does physics end and astronomy begin?

If a scientist uses physics to calculate the orbit of Jupiter, and chemistry to determine the gases in the planet's atmosphere, is this scientist a physicist, a chemist, or an astronomer?

That is how our minds seem to be developing. All our models are slowly merging into a single large one.

Here is an interesting possibility, Chris. I do not know this for a fact, but I suspect that the process of eliminating contradictions and merging our small models into one large one is the process of acquiring **wisdom.**

One reason this seems likely to me is that as we improve our models and learn new ones, the models shed light on each other, as in the case of physics, chemistry, and astronomy.

Also, as we learn more, we also become aware of how much we do not know. This makes us broadminded, willing to see things from another person's point of view.

That makes us reluctant to encroach on other people and more comfortable allowing them to live their lives in their own ways.

Sounds like wisdom to me.

Uncle Eric

17

How to Get Started
Learning Models

Dear Chris,

To be successful, you must understand the world in which you live. There are four models I suggest you study deeply. These are not the last word on the subject, but in my experience they are good places to start, and these four models will provide a practical foundation.

The first model is a business model. I will get into that in Section Two of this set of letters.

The second is an economic model. As I said in an earlier letter, the economic model I believe sheds the most light on the events that affect us is called Austrian economics (called this because the founders were from Austria). Austrian economics is the economic model that most closely dovetails with the principles on which America was founded.

Chris, I will present the Austrian economic view in three different sets of letters. I mentioned the first set of letters to you earlier, the set I call WHATEVER HAPPENED TO PENNY CANDY? I will also write two additional sets of letters that I'll call THE

MONEY MYSTERY and THE CLIPPER SHIP STRATEGY[19]. These three sets of letters will give you a lot of guidance on how to manage your business, career, and investments to achieve maximum possible success with minimum risk.

The third model is a legal model. The legal model that most closely agrees with Austrian economics and includes the principles on which America was founded is the old British common law. I will present the old British common law view in three different sets of letters. I mentioned the first set of letters to you earlier, the set I call WHATEVER HAPPENED TO JUSTICE? I will also write two additional sets of letters that I'll call ANCIENT ROME: HOW IT AFFECTS YOU TODAY, and ARE YOU LIBERAL, CONSERVATIVE OR CONFUSED?[20]

Fourth is the foreign policy model, meaning the guidelines for the U.S. Government's relations with other nations. I will present the foreign policy model in three different sets of letters about war. The first set will be called: THE THOUSAND YEAR WAR IN THE MIDEAST: HOW IT AFFECTS YOU TODAY, followed by WORLD WAR I: THE REST OF THE STORY AND HOW IT AFFECTS YOU TODAY, and WORLD WAR II: THE REST OF THE STORY AND HOW IT AFFECTS YOU TODAY.[21]

---

[19] THE MONEY MYSTERY and THE CLIPPER SHIP STRATEGY by Richard J. Maybury are both published by Bluestocking Press, www.BluestockingPress.com; Phone: 800-959-8586.

[20] ANCIENT ROME: HOW IT AFFECTS YOU TODAY and ARE YOU LIBERAL? CONSERVATIVE? OR CONFUSED? by Richard J. Maybury are both published by Bluestocking Press, www.BluestockingPress.com; Phone: 800-959-8586.

[21] THE THOUSAND YEAR WAR IN THE MIDEAST: HOW IT AFFECTS YOU TODAY, WORLD WAR I: THE REST OF THE STORY AND HOW IT AFFECTS YOU TODAY, and WORLD WAR II: THE REST OF THE STORY AND HOW IT AFFECTS YOU TODAY by Richard J. Maybury are all published by Bluestocking Press, www.BluestockingPress.com; Phone: 800-959-8586.

I am not saying I think these four models are infallible, or that they are the last word on their subjects. They are what I have found to be most useful at this time.

Chris, before we move on to Part Two, I should summarize what I have written so far. This summary will be brief because you will receive a more detailed one at the end of this set of letters. Here it is.

Models, or paradigms, are how we understand our world. In my opinion, Chris, models are the most important concept you will ever learn because they are the basis of all other concepts.

Fortunately, models are also the simplest concept to learn. We all build and modify our models every day, automatically. Even toddlers, babies, dogs, and cats build simple models without realizing what they are doing.

My main point is, be aware you are building models and try to build good ones.

If someone offers you new information, or a new model, then a logical question to ask is, what model was used to prove this?

Chris, now that you understand models, you have an extremely useful intellectual tool that few others do. I look forward to hearing about the ways in which you use this tool, and I hope that you will share what you have learned with the people you care about.

Uncle Eric

P.S. An interesting question is: How much of our models are formed consciously and how much unconsciously?

It is hard to say. It might depend on the model.

For instance, when you are learning archery, you concentrate very hard on using the right form when holding the bow, aiming, and releasing. You practice this form over and over, deliberately trying to infuse it into your "muscle memory." This is a case of consciously adopting a model.

When a child is taught to tie his shoe, the learning is a laborious process requiring great concentration. After a few months, the child can tie the shoe without thinking about it. The child does not know about models, but the model of a tied shoe, and the method for achieving it, has been absorbed.

I think most or all models start out as conscious efforts, then slip into the unconscious. This is what we call "developing a habit." Once the model has been adopted, the mind follows the programming, the internal map, without knowing this is what it is doing. Also, once the muscle memory work becomes automatic, the mind is free to move on to another challenge.

If you agree, Chris, I suggest you begin to be aware of how many models you have already adopted without realizing it.

Are they all good ones?

Part Two

The Best Model for Success

18

What is Success?

Dear Chris,

Now that you know about models, we will begin getting into the how-to, nuts-and-bolts of making models work for you.

How does one achieve success in her or his business, career, and investments?

First let's define success. There are many kinds — success in love, success in sports, success in horse training, and on and on.

What we will be talking about is success with money, in your business, career, and investments. What is the best model for earning money and for keeping it?

In my next several letters I will write about earning it, then in my final letters about keeping it.

Let's get started.

For our purposes here, I will divide economic groups into seven classes: lower, lower middle, middle middle, upper middle, affluent, wealthy, and super wealthy.

Throughout all of history until the 1800s, everyone was, by our standards today, lower class, meaning poor. Today it is possible for nearly anyone to become middle class, and most Americans are. Middle middle class is achievable by having a high school diploma, getting a job with a good company, and being hard working and honest.

Nothing wrong with that, but in these letters I am trying to show you how to achieve something more. I want you to have enough money to take vacations abroad; live in a large, comfortable, modern home; have two late model cars; excellent medical care; send your children to college; and have a comfortable, enjoyable retirement. These are characteristics of the upper middle class and the affluent class.

It is also possible, of course, to get into the wealthy or super wealthy classes. I think it is more realistic, however, to shoot for the upper middle class or, hopefully, affluence. I want you to have an abundance of all the material things you might want, but I'm not going to try to get you into a mansion and personal jet. When working the long, hard hours required for that level of success, the risks to one's personal life can be extreme. Some can overcome these risks, but that is rare.

Physical, emotional, and spiritual health, and loving relationships are far more important than money. But, a big income can make these more important things easier to achieve and easier to keep.

In other words, material things are not the so-called good life, but they can help you get to the good life, and they can make it easier for you to help others get there. (Which is what I am trying to do for you.)

In case you have not learned this yet, Chris, helping others can be a great source of satisfaction, and, if you have money, you can do a lot more of it.

Uncle Eric

19

A Short History
of Models for Success

Dear Chris,

How does one achieve success in business, career, and investments?

That question has been one of the most important people have asked since the beginning of history. The short answer is: find a model that works. Here is the long answer.

Originally — I'm going back thousands of years here — there were two models. One was to work for the king, warlord, pharaoh, emperor, or whatever the local ruler was called. Governments have the legal privilege of taking money via taxation — so a person who worked for one of these rulers always had a more secure income than those who did not. The higher this person rose in the government — meaning the more closely he worked with the head ruler — the more financially secure he would be.

The other model for success was to own a business.

Until the **Industrial Revolution**[22] began in the 1700s, a business was, in most cases, a farm. Sometimes it would be

---

[22] Industrial Revolution: beginning in the 1700s, the use of machines for mass production of goods.

a store or a workshop of some kind, but for most of history, I am sure at least 90% of the businesses were farms.

The way the model worked was, get a job as an employee of a business, save your money, and then use your savings (your "capital") to start or buy your own business. This is called capitalizing the business.

The person who starts, owns, and runs a business is an **entrepreneur**. (On-tra-pra-newer.)

The reason owning a business was the surest honorable route to success was that, when times were good, the owner of the business earned more than any of the employees; and, when times were bad, the owner was the last person to lose his job.

Chris, one reason the owner of a business earns more than anyone else in the firm is that he has his own money at risk. He buys the farm or shop and the equipment in it, and stands to lose these assets if the business goes broke.

Also, the owner typically works longer hours than anyone else, at least until he has built the business up to the point that he can hire managers to run it.

In America, owning a business was by far the surest route to financial security because until the 20th century the government was very small and did not hire many people. Most Americans had only two choices, own a private business or be an employee of a private business.

By the 20th century, however, the Industrial Revolution had made businesses so productive that an employee could earn very good wages — good enough, in fact, to live far better than any of his ancestors.

By 1950, the typical American assembly line worker had better medical care, more nutritious food, faster and more comfortable transportation, far more entertainment, and a great many other things that were much superior to anything previous generations had dreamed of. This worker was so well off he lived better than a medieval king, better than a Roman emperor.

Imagine. This employee could have orange juice in winter. If his vision was blurry, he could have eyeglasses. He could talk with friends over distances of hundreds of miles. He could even ride in comfort down a broad artificial stone road, speeding along at a mile a minute.

For most of history, such miracles were thought to be impossible, but suddenly, in the 20th century, after all the thousands of years of human history, it was possible to be financially successful and comfortable by working for someone else — by being an employee.

Amazing. The business owner model no longer stood alone. Now the new 20th century employee model produced good results, too. We can call this the **prosperous employee model.**

The prosperous employee model worked for perhaps seventy years — roughly 1900 to 1970 — so most American adults who are alive today grew up with it and lived with it long enough to assume this model had always existed. Few know enough economic history to realize how new and different the prosperous employee model is — or was.

I say "was" because, I believe, for all practical purposes the prosperous employee model is gone.

By 1980, the possibility of getting a good job with a solid company, then working one's way up in the company, earning ever-higher wages until retiring as a member of the upper middle or affluent class, had evaporated away. Millions who were faithfully following this model found that progress had become very difficult, and many were going backward.

What happened?
I will explain in my next letter.

Uncle Eric

20

Another Mouth to Feed

Dear Chris,

Why did the prosperous employee model go away?

We cannot be certain, the study of human behavior is a very inexact science, but in my opinion, the biggest fly in the ointment was the fast growing government.

In a word, taxes. Taxes are one of the prices we pay for government.

Until the 20th century, the U.S. Government was so small it was supported by import taxes and taxes on liquor and tobacco. There was no income tax until 1913.[23] It is very difficult for us to imagine a government that small and inexpensive.

This comparison might help: Today, the state and local government in Ohio alone is larger than the entire federal government was, including the armed forces, until 1915.[24]

Prior to the 20th century, the U.S. government had grown larger, especially during the Civil War, and then its growth

---

[23] A temporary income tax had been levied to pay for the Civil War.

[24] Measured by number of employees. Sources: HISTORICAL STATISTICS OF THE US, and STATISTICAL ABSTRACT OF THE US.

became very rapid during World War I, which began in 1914. Then in the Great Depression of the 1930s, and World War II, its growth became explosive.

So did the taxes needed to support it.

By 1980, in most wage-earning families, government had become another mouth to feed, the largest mouth.

In 1950, the average American family paid about two percent of its income in federal taxes. By 1995, the family was paying 24 percent.[25]

State and local taxes had gone up a lot, too, so government was consuming at least 30 percent of the average family's income, and in millions of cases more than 40 percent.

That's the monetary burden. There is also a time burden. Each year, Americans spend millions of hours filling out tax forms and maintaining their tax records.

Chris, get a ruler, I want to show you something. In 1952, the manual containing the federal tax code was three-fourths of an inch thick, and the tax regulations, another half-inch, for a total of one and a quarter inches. Mark that with your thumbnail. These pages listed the federal tax laws Americans were required to obey.

By the year 2000, the code and regulations together were fourteen inches thick.[26]

Each year the Internal Revenue Service sends out eight *billion* pages of forms and instructions, and the paperwork received each year by the IRS would circle the earth 36 times.[27]

---

[25] "Renewing American Civilization," U.S. News & World Report, 15 May 95, p.46.

[26] "Is This Progress," Wall Street Journal, 28 May 97, p.1.

[27] Heritage Foundation Backgrounder, number 1107, April 2, 1997, p.3.

The long hours each family is forced to spend filling out these tax forms and keeping tax records is a time tax. These are hours parents cannot use to earn income to support their children or to do any number of other important things.

Personally, I spend about two weeks each year keeping tax records and filling out tax forms. If my adult life turns out to be sixty years long, this means I will have spent more than two full years of my life doing tax paperwork.

In 1950, the typical American family was a husband, wife, and children, with the husband working outside the home and the wife working inside.

It was taken for granted that the family could get ahead with only one parent working an outside job.

By the year 2000, both parents typically worked outside the home, and the equivalent of one parent's income went entirely to pay federal, state, and local taxes.

In other words, by the year 2000, one parent worked to support the family, and the other worked to support the government.

In 1970, the typical American family was saving about nine percent of its income.[28] By the year 2000, the savings rate was down to near zero.[29] The prosperous employee model was dead.

The result, Chris, is that today it takes a lot more income to get into the upper middle class and stay there. In my

---

[28] Income remaining after taxes. Economists call this Personal Savings as a Percent of Disposable Income.

[29] These are percentages of Disposable Personal Income, meaning income remaining after taxes. "U.S. Savings Rate Hits an All-Time Low," Wall Street Journal, 29 Aug 00, p.A2.

opinion, the only realistic way to earn this income is to own a good business.

Uncle Eric

P.S. An interesting question, Chris: if one parent is working outside the home to support the family, and the other is working outside the home to support the government, how much time is left to raise the children?

Personal Savings Rate
Savings as a percent of after-tax income

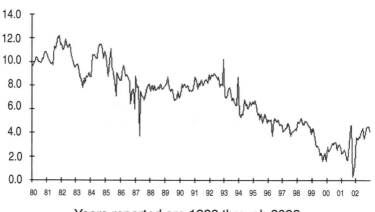

Years reported are 1980 through 2002

21

A Model Born of Desperation

Dear Chris,

There are still people who make the employee model work. With two adults laboring outside the home, the family makes good progress; they get ahead.

Financially.[30]

Except for a few rare cases, the only people I know who have made this model work well are those without children.

Most can afford to support children, or they can afford to support the government; they cannot afford to support both.

If they try, something or someone gets neglected. Maybe it is the children, or maybe the marriage, or one's own self. But something is left behind.

Again, there are exceptions, but in my experience, these exceptions are rare.

By the 1990s, millions of wage earners realized they were facing a bleak future. Their standard of living was high, but it was precarious and threatening to plunge backward.

---

[30] Getting ahead financially means their net worth increases — the total value of their savings and all other property rises year after year.

Looking for a way to make big money fast, millions who knew very little about economics or finance began pouring their money into the stock market.

Under this new demand, prices of stocks rose strongly. The age-old dream of making big money without working appeared to have come true.

Seeing their friends raking in the dough, millions more piled into the stock market, bidding prices up to insane levels.

Chris, much of the country was swept by a kind of euphoria. People were thrilled to see they could get ahead without relying on the prosperous employee model. The stock market would make them rich, without working.

I call this the get-rich-quick investment model. As in the 1920s, this model did work for a few — those who got into the stock market early and got out before the bubble burst.

But most did not get out in time, and by 2002, euphoria had turned to misery, as the market fell and millions saw their savings disappear, their hopes destroyed.

Knowing little about economic history, most did not realize that this kind of easy-riches mania has happened often, and always with the same result: get-rich-quick has turned to get-poor-quick.

Equally important, investors lost time. During the 1990s, they had poured their energy into speculation instead of productive work, losing time they could have used in more rewarding ways.

So, Chris, today the prosperous employee model is gone, and the get-rich-quick investment model has failed, too.

In my opinion, we are back to where we were before the 20th century. The only reliable model for achieving substantial wealth and security is to own a healthy business.

The most important word here is *healthy*. How do you make your business healthy, and how do you keep it that way? My next letter.

Uncle Eric

22

Making Your Model Work

Dear Chris,

This will be a long letter. There are a lot of things you need to know to make a business healthy. I will give you a list.

It takes time to learn these skills — for some skills, ten minutes, for others ten months — but a major additional benefit is that most of these sets of knowledge will do double-duty for you. They will not only help make your business successful, they will help you run your private life more smoothly and with fewer problems.

Much of this you can get in high school or college courses, or by independent study. I will make suggestions about books to read.

Some will require hands-on work experience, and I will offer ways to acquire that.

When learning something in a classroom, always talk with the instructor before you sign up for a class, to make sure he or she will cover the specific topics you want to learn.

As you are learning, be aware of the models you are assembling in your mind. Also try to determine the model your instructor will be using.

Let me warn you, Chris, some of my suggestions will be rather unconventional. This is because I am not trying to steer you in the direction of a course of study that would be recommended by most schools and colleges. I am trying to give you the rest of the story, knowledge that is generally acquired from the "school of hard knocks," however, I'm trying to save you from the knocks. I want to help you become "street-wise" about how the world really works.

Lest this list overwhelm you at first, let me say that by no means do I expect you to study/do each of the things I suggest right away. It took me years to acquire this body of knowledge. By itemizing what I think is important for success I only hope to expedite the process for you. At the very least, I would like you to become familiar with my suggestions now so that you can start exploring your options. These studies are listed in no particular order and I do not think you need to go through them in any order. After you have finished the rest of my sets of "Uncle Eric" letters[31] just go work through this list in the order that is most convenient to you.

I suggest you get a pencil or highlighter. As I make suggestions, underline or highlight the books you plan to read, the school courses you plan to take, and the jobs you plan to get. This underlining/highlighting will be your plan for achieving success in your business, career, and investments.

---

[31] Uncle Eric is referring to the rest of the "Uncle Eric" books written by Richard J. Maybury and published by Bluestocking Press, web site: www.BluestockingPress.com

Jobs/Internships

Chris, here is something very important. Young people who first enter the workplace, or are working their way through college, usually have a succession of entry-level and part-time jobs. Most, in searching for these jobs, look only for something that pays well and is, hopefully, not too boring.

Crucial to success, I believe, is to have lots of these early jobs, and make them part of your education.

Select your jobs as carefully as you would select college courses, so that they give you important experience as well as money.

And, once you have learned as much as you can from a job, move on to the next one. Where appropriate, I will mention the kind of job that will give you the needed experience.

Indeed, Chris, if I had it to do over again, knowing what I now know, I would not see these jobs as jobs; I would see them as courses of study for which you get paid.

Looking back over my life, I realize that if I had begun this course of study when I was your age, I probably would have achieved success twenty years earlier than I did. It is too late for me, those twenty years are gone, but not for you, Chris, so I hope you give it your best shot.

Chris, it might take a lot of research to find a job that will give you the learning experience you're looking for. However, many tools are available to help you. At the time I write this, Internet sites allow you to enter specific criteria to conduct your job search. Colleges have career centers. These centers exist to help students find jobs/internships in their fields of study, learn how to write a good resume, what to do in interviews, how to "dress for success," and more.

Business Degree Courses

Chris, the skills I list in this segment are vital for any entrepreneur. Most business degree programs train students to be managers in large corporations. However, if you go into business for yourself you will still benefit from the knowledge learned in these courses.

If you do not major in business, I strongly recommend getting a basic, working knowledge of these subjects, which will help you manage your own business and finances, as well as aid greatly in helping you understand how the world works. Even if you don't go to college to earn a degree, you can take advantage of community college courses, in the subjects you need to study. In many cases, you can locate a textbook and self-study. In some instances, however, a good instructor and/or classroom experience will be a tremendous benefit over self-study.

Accounting

This is one of the most essential skills for success in running a business and your private life. Be able to keep a full set of paper-and-pencil books using double-entry bookkeeping. After you can do it on paper, then it is okay to go to a computer, but not before; you need to understand what the computer is doing. Be good at reading a balance sheet and income statement. A good place to get this knowledge is in high school or college courses. This is one of those instances when it is especially helpful to have an instructor correct your work and answer your questions.

Finance

Know a lot about the nuts and bolts of financial instruments such as stocks, bonds, options, commodities, insurance, mortgages, Treasury-bills, and certificates of deposit. Know enough that you can allocate your **portfolio** yourself without advice from others. Information from others is good, but advice on allocation can get you into big trouble because most financial experts do not know enough about economics or geopolitics to understand how these forces affect investments. (You will learn a lot about these forces in my future letters.) Learn to do it yourself. Especially know a lot about interest rates and **opportunity costs**. A good place to get the nuts and bolts of finance is high school and college personal finance courses. Before taking the courses, talk with the instructors to be sure they will teach what you need to know to keep your money safe. Safety is a lot more important than profits; it is much easier to keep money than to replace it.

Personal Selling (Selling Face-To-Face)

Chris, no matter what you do in life, sales skills will be important for success. Even if you decide to be a career employee, you will still need to sell yourself to employers when you are interviewing for jobs. If your sales skills are good, your career choices will be greater.

Speaking of choices, to get someone to buy what you are trying to sell you really have two choices. The first, as exemplified by films about the mafia, uses force to make someone buy what is being sold. The second choice uses peaceful persuasion, which requires sales ability. Obviously, the latter will keep you healthier longer and is also legal. Remember, selling is the alternative to brute force.

Good selling skills are one of the most important routes to financial security; if you can sell, you can always earn money.

At bottom, selling is a simple process. Find out what the customer wants and then find a way to supply it. The exact procedures for doing this, however, can be challenging.

I have no objections to taking courses in sales, but they will not be enough. In sales, there is no substitute for hands-on experience.

A job selling shoes, flowers, or auto parts would be fine, but selling large appliances, cars, or in-ground swimming pools would be better. The more expensive the item, the more commission[32] you are likely to earn. And, more importantly, big-ticket items have more complex selling processes, so you will learn more.

In my opinion, the most satisfying sales jobs are those that involve selling to businesses rather than ordinary consumers. The typical business decision maker is, I believe, better informed and more logical than the typical consumer, so emotion plays a smaller part in the selling process.

The ordinary consumer is famously emotional, so a sales person who sells to consumers must appeal to this emotion. The selling process can be messy, and it sometimes leads to dishonest behavior on both sides of the transaction.

Sales people who sell to businesses are mostly consultants who know they must emphasize cold, hard facts if they wish to make the sale.

---

[32] Commission: a percentage of the selling price paid to the sales person.

Granted, even to large corporations, the final decision always has an emotional component — the final decision makers are all human — but usually the emotional component in business sales is much less than in consumer sales.

Read the book SPIN SELLING by Neil Rackham. Half of all America's top companies, meaning the so-called Fortune 500, use SPIN selling.

Then look for a selling job. I suggest that you tell the person who interviews you that you want the job because you want to learn how to be good at sales.

Finding out what the customer (or prospective employer) wants may sound like an easy process, but often it is not. What the customer (or employer) *says* he wants may not be what he *really* wants; you need to learn how to get to the truth of the matter. If possible, select an employer who will give you extensive training in sales.

Advertising

Along the same lines, the most difficult type of selling is through direct response written advertising — for instance, a magazine ad that tries to persuade the customer to respond directly to the advertiser by phone, mail, or internet, rather than persuading a customer who comes to a store.

Direct response advertising is difficult because you cannot talk directly with the customer. You must anticipate his questions and objections, and answer them, usually all in a very small space.

Fundamental to all sales is the fact that the customer is always saying to himself, I am being asked to trade my hard-earned money for this, so what will it do for me? Your ads must prove to the customer that the benefits will be worth the costs.

This points to what may be the most important concept in sales, the difference between features and benefits. When trying to sell something, or apply for a job, we tend to talk about features.

The customer (or employer) wants to hear about benefits.

A feature answers the question, what is the product?

A benefit answers the question, what will it do for me?

A book recommended to me by one of the top ad writers in America is HOW TO WRITE A GOOD ADVERTISEMENT — A SHORT COURSE IN COPYRIGHTING by Victor O. Schwab.

The multimillionaire ad writer told me Schwab's book was a highly important key to the ad writer's success. I read it, and it contributed in no small part to my own success. I am sure this will be one of the most important books you will ever read.

Chris, if I had to pick the one book most likely to give you financial security for the rest of your life, HOW TO WRITE A GOOD ADVERTISEMENT might be it. If you can write successful direct response ads, you will have climbed the Mt. Everest of sales, and there will be almost no limit to the amount of money you can earn. Because this skill is so important, I have put together the following as a model for a written ad.

A Model for Writing Ads

An ad is in five parts:

1. Headline. The purpose of the headline is to grab the reader's attention and draw him in, nothing else. It should provoke curiosity.

2. Features. The purpose of the features is to give the reader a description of the product. He only needs enough features to know what you are talking about. Too many features bog him down in detail.

3. Benefits. The purpose of the benefits is to tell the reader why he needs the product. The benefits must be strong enough to justify the price. The more benefits the better, it's not possible to have too many. If you cannot think of enough to justify the price, then this is a sign you need a better product.

4. Close. The purpose of the close is to tell the reader to buy. The more times you close him, the more likely the sale.

5. Urgency. Create urgency; tell the reader to buy right *now*, and give him a reason to do so because in most cases a sale delayed is a sale lost.

Incidentally, Chris, notice that this five-step process is also the one you will use when applying for jobs.

1. Get the employer's attention.

2. Tell him who you are and what your abilities are.

3. Explain how beneficial you will be to him.

4. Say directly, "Can I have this job?"

5. Then politely tell him that you won't be available forever; if he wants you he must make you an offer now.

Chris, here is an example ad derived from the model. In this example, features are underlined, *benefits* are in script, and **closes** are bolded. Note that this brief ad contains 12 benefits and 6 closes.

You Need This Car!

The <u>four-door</u> Backfire Z99 station wagon comes standard equipped with one of the *highest fidelity* <u>AM,FM,CD stereos</u> you have ever heard. The <u>eight speakers</u> *let you relish every note from each instrument, with crystal clarity.* Whether you prefer jazz, country and western, or classical, this stereo will *make you look forward to getting behind the wheel.* **Start enjoying** beautiful sounds **today, take a Backfire home with you now.**

The Z99's <u>cargo compartment</u> is a full <u>five feet long and three feet high</u>, to let you *carry outsize loads that will not fit in an ordinary sedan.* **Drive your new Backfire to a lumberyard or sporting goods store tomorrow** and see the *huge load it can carry.*

The <u>four-wheel disk brakes</u> and <u>radial tires</u> provide one of the *safest* rides available anywhere. Insurance company studies rate Backfires as one of the most *invulnerable* cars in their class.

A Z99's upholstery is *plush* <u>leather,</u> *soft and sensuous* to the touch, but <u>specially treated</u> to be *stain resistant* and *easy to clean.*

To make it simple for you to **get into your own Z99 today,** we offer special discount pricing for a limited time only. **Sign the papers, pick up the keys**, and **feel your turbocharged four-liter engine whisk you away** to many years of driving *pleasure.*

Chris, advertising is one of those cases where there is no substitute for hands-on experience. After you read HOW TO WRITE A GOOD ADVERTISEMENT, I suggest a part-time job in an ad agency. This connects to my next two suggestions, printing and photography, which are not business degree courses, but I include them here because of their connection to advertising.

Printing

Printed material is one of the most valuable and under-rated tools of every successful business. Let me emphasize, *every* business uses printed material. I suggest a part-time job in a print shop so you can learn the language of the print trade, and learn how to carry a full-color job with photos all the way from layout to finished product. You don't need to be become a master at printing, but learn how printing is done and how printing projects can be completed most economically.

Photography

This is not only an enjoyable hobby, it can also be invaluable in sales and in producing printed material. Humans are sight-oriented, they want visual images. The better you are at giving this to them, the more successful you can be. A picture is worth a thousand words.

Until you have become proficient at photography, avoid fully automatic point-and-shoot cameras, they won't teach you much. A high school or college course that teaches how to use a basic (non-automatic) 35 mm single-lens reflex camera will help you learn the essentials of lighting, composition, film types, etc.

Computer Spreadsheets and Databases

It is almost impossible to be successful in any field without a steady supply of high quality information and ways to analyze it. No matter what you do in life, you will probably be working with computer spreadsheets and databases, or the tables, charts, and other outputs from these programs. A good high school or college course should teach you all you need to know.

Algebra

Be a wiz at writing formulas that generate insightful graphics from computer spread sheets. Look for a good high school or college course. I do not think your algebra needs to be very advanced, unless you are going into a technical field as a profession, but you should be highly proficient in the basics. In my opinion, the best books available to teach you these basics are INTRODUCTORY ALGEBRA and INTERMEDIATE ALGEBRA, written by head author Margaret Lial. As I write this, Bluestocking Press is distributing these books, as well as a very excellent BUSINESS MATHEMATICS book. You can check Bluestocking Press' web site for current information at www.BluestockingPress.com.

Statistics

Chris, all your life you will be dealing with statistics, so it is a good idea to take a course in it. Also, I recommend the revealing little book HOW TO LIE WITH STATISTICS, by Darrell Huff.

Business Law

Law is one of the most important subjects you will ever learn, and you will get an introduction to it in my set of letters I call WHATEVER HAPPENED TO JUSTICE?

Chris, it is not necessary to be a lawyer, but you do need to know a lot about contracts, as well as other legal subjects. Be familiar with the Uniform Commercial Code, which you should be able to find in several places on the Internet. Do a Google™ search.

An essential reference book for your personal library is BLACK'S LAW DICTIONARY. I also suggest HANDBOOK OF EVERYDAY LAW, by Gordon Coughlin, Jr., and you can find other laymen's guides to law in any large bookstore.

Perhaps the best way to learn about law is a college course or two in Business Law, but be careful. It has been my experience that many of these courses are not well taught, and they use poor textbooks.

Before you sign up, talk with the instructor to make sure you will get a solid understanding of contracts and property, and a familiarity with the Uniform Commercial Code. Also, the course should make heavy use of case studies, either real or fictional.

Public Speaking

Public speaking is essential, especially presentation skills. You cannot self-study public speaking. You have to get out there and do it. The organization called Toastmasters might do a better job for you than a college course. Check the Yellow Pages under Public Speaking and the White Pages under Toastmasters. Learn to work with an overhead projector,

PowerPoint slides, and other visual aids. Do enough speeches to get over stage fright. And speaking of stage fright, learn how to adlib and improvise so you become comfortable with the unexpected. You can learn how to do this in drama classes and by participating in community theatre. Drama and presentation speaking each provide benefits that the other does not, so try to participate in both.

Business Writing

Learn to write letters, reports, and proposals. A high school or college course might be a good way. Make sure you are doing a lot of actual writing, as opposed to studying theory. When you were a small child, the way you learned to speak was by speaking. Practice. The best way to learn to write well is to write, and write, and write. If you keep a journal, by writing 500 words per day about anything that comes to mind, you will find your writing skills much improved in just three months.

Subjects for Self-Study

Geopolitics

Geopolitics means world politics. Your business, career, and investments will be highly dependent on the economy. What happens in the economy is strongly influenced by politics — and national politics is strongly influenced by geopolitics.

An example of the importance of geopolitics occurred in early 2003, when companies became reluctant to buy new equipment or hire workers, and investors became afraid to buy stocks because they were worried about President Bush invading Iraq. It was a considerable mess that drastically changed flows of money.

In other words, events on the other side of the world often hit us in our wallets harder than events in our hometowns.

Americans generally do not study geopolitics — most probably don't even have the word in their vocabularies — so in the U.S., a knowledge of geopolitics can give you a sizable edge (as well as a lot of prestige, if you want it).

You will get a great deal of geopolitics as you read more of my letters (especially those I call ANCIENT ROME and the three war books I mentioned earlier, THE THOUSAND YEAR WAR, WORLD WAR I, and WORLD WAR II). In those letters I will give you suggestions on where to learn more, assuming you wish to do so.

Chris, after you have finished all my sets of letters, you should subscribe to a publication that will give you high quality geopolitical news in language you can easily understand. I recommend THE ECONOMIST magazine. Any large library should have copies, and these will contain subscription information.

Again, Chris, it is hard to overemphasize the importance of the fact that events on the other side of the world often affect our wallets more than events in our hometowns. Study geopolitics.

Directly related to geopolitics is military affairs.

Military Affairs

Chris, it is sad but true that the strongest influence on your business, career, and investments will be government — both the U.S. Government and foreign governments — and the most important aspect of governmental behavior is the use of military force. Wars and threats of war change flows of money, which means they blindside people who are not paying attention, and they create opportunities for those who are.

This is generally not well understood, which is why so many people are caught off guard by major geopolitical events. They simply are not equipped to see what is headed their way.

Chris, the overwhelmingly important influence of military affairs is why it is crucially important to know something about weapons, strategy, tactics, logistics, and previous wars, especially the world wars and the Vietnam War. History repeats. It never repeats exactly, but close enough for us to detect warning signs.

You do not need to like war or military affairs, but you need to know about them. If you pay attention to news about economics and investments, you have probably noticed that after September 11, 2001 (also referred to as 9-11),[33] the economy, the investment markets, and the war all merged into a single story.

---

[33] On September 11, 2001, in an attack against the United States, over 3000 civilians were murdered. The World Trade Center in New York was destroyed, as well as a portion of the Pentagon. Four civilian airliners were destroyed, including their passengers and crew. This attack is also referred to as Sept. 11, Sept. 11 Attack, and 9-11.

You will find some military information in my future sets of letters, and a baffling amount in any large bookstore. However, you are not likely to find a formal classroom course, so, after you have finished reading my future letters, here are my suggestions for your own do-it-yourself course in military studies:

DIRTY LITTLE SECRETS — MILITARY INFORMATION YOU'RE NOT SUPPOSED TO KNOW, by James F. Dunnigan and Albert A. Nofi. Published in 1990, this book is somewhat out of date, but nevertheless packed with fascinating tidbits about weapons, strategy, and geopolitics. It contains lots of insights here that no government wants you to have.

THE OXFORD BOOK OF MILITARY ANECDOTES, edited by Max Hastings. Persons who have not served in the armed forces sometimes have misleading notions about what military life and warfare are really like. This collection of short stories from the experiences of troops and officers will dispel any notions about glory, precision, heroism, or effectiveness. War is, more than anything else, chaos.

SUPPLYING WAR, by Martin van Creveld. An old saying among generals and admirals is that amateurs talk about strategy while experts talk about logistics. Logistics is the ability to get bullets and beans to the troops. Creveld believes logistics is 90% of warfare, and I would not disagree. Understand logistics and you understand a great deal about how war affects the economy and the investment markets, too.

Chris, nearly all wars today are guerrilla[34] wars, and the "war on terrorism," is no exception. "Special operations," which mostly means anti-guerrilla warfare, is the point of the spear. The next two books give you a look at the weapons, tactics, and a bit of strategy in special operations.

SHADOW WARRIORS: INSIDE THE SPECIAL FORCES, by Tom Clancy.

THE COMPLETE IDIOT'S GUIDE TO U.S. SPECIAL OPS FORCES, by Marc Cerasini.

Tom Clancy is famously knowledgeable about military affairs, and his series of books about the various parts of the U.S. armed forces will give you more than you will ever need to know. These books are: ARMORED CAV, CARRIER, SUBMARINE, FIGHTER WING, MARINE, and AIRBORNE.

VIETNAM, A HISTORY, THE FIRST COMPLETE ACCOUNT OF THE VIETNAM WAR, by Stanley Karnow, gives the whole awful story about the Vietnam War and, therefore, a lot of insight into why the Pentagon is so afraid of guerrilla war.

BLOWBACK, by Chalmers Johnson. Invented by the CIA, the term "blowback" refers to the revenge foreigners exact for the federal government's (often secret) meddling in their countries. I hope you will make this highly useful term part of your vocabulary.

---

[34] Guerrilla: an "irregular" or part-time soldier, usually a volunteer who wears civilian clothes and operates by stealth, without a formal command structure.

I suggest you ignore Johnson's leftist economics; but in my opinion, his geopolitics is perfectly on target.

A HISTORY OF WARFARE, by John Keegan, is an encyclopedic look at the evolution of warfare since ancient times, including hardware, strategy, and tactics. It includes many insights about how war affects the psychology of a leader to the point that the leader does not steer the war, the war steers the leader.

THE PRINCE, by Niccolo Machiavelli. When using his power, a politician can experience a high much like that produced by cocaine. If he is a power addict, he does not own his power, his power owns him; he dances to its tune.

> "I have thought it proper to represent things as they are in real truth, rather than as they are imagined. ... I know everyone will agree that it would be most laudable if a prince possessed all the qualities deemed to be good among those I have enumerated. But, because of conditions in the world, princes cannot have these qualities."

So wrote Machiavelli in THE PRINCE, published in 1532. This short book remains the most revealing explanation of how governments really work, and no government on earth wants you to read it. It is packed with insight that will keep you from jumping to high-risk conclusions about how government will affect your business, career, and investments.

Chris, you will find THE PRINCE especially helpful in understanding foreign and military policies. It is so savvy about political power that it was a favorite book of Italian dictator Benito Mussolini. So, if you want to be streetwise about what governments really are, and how they really behave, read THE PRINCE.

By the way, I recommend the Penguin Classics edition of THE PRINCE translated by George Bull; the introduction is not to be missed.

Constitutional Law

Understand Constitutional law, especially the Bill of Rights, and some criminal law, as well as probable cause and related concepts. You should get these in introductory political science courses and law courses, but after you take them, also do some reading on your own. I recommend any book about law or the Constitution sold by the following:

Bluestocking Press
PO Box 1014
Dept. TA2
Placerville, CA 95667-1014
(800) 959-8586
www.BluestockingPress.com

Cato Institute
1000 Massachusetts Avenue, N.W.
Washington D.C. 20001-5403
Phone (202) 842-0200; Fax (202) 842-3490

Foundation for Economic Education
30 S. Broadway
Irvington-on-Hudson, NY 10533.
(800) 960-4FEE
www.fee.org

The Independent Institute
100 Swan Way
Oakland, CA 94621-1428
Phone (800) 927-8733 or (510) 632-1366
Fax: (510) 568-6040
www.liberty-tree.org

Laissez Faire Books
7123 Interstate 30, Suite 42
Little Rock, AR 72209
(800) 326-0996
www.lfb.com

Economics

Chris, it is essential to understand enough economics to be able to locate customers, determine where your customers get their money, and how stable their incomes are; *you* earn money only if *they* earn money.

Even if you spend the rest of your life as an employee, it is still crucially important to be able to see how stable your employer's income is, so that you can safely plan ahead. For instance, should you put your savings into a new house, or are you in danger of being laid off? If you have a choice, should you contribute to your employer's pension fund or make your own investment decisions? Or, should you work for an employer that gives you no choice about how your contributions to a retirement fund are being invested?

You will get a sizable dose of this kind of understanding in my three sets of letters about economics, WHATEVER HAPPENED TO PENNY CANDY?, THE MONEY MYSTERY, AND THE CLIPPER SHIP STRATEGY. These contain suggestions for further reading, and I recommend anything sold by the firms listed under Constitutional law. I did not list economics under the "Business Degree" segment, although you will be required to take economics as a business major. However, beware that the courses taught at most colleges focus on Keynesian economics, *not* free-market, (Austrian and Monetarist) economics. If you must study Keynesian economics in college, first read my three sets of letters about economics, so you are well-grounded in free-market economics. Only a handful of colleges teach the model of free-market economics, so, unless you plan to attend one of those, you will need to self-study free-market economics.

Economic History

Economic history is extremely important because it helps you develop a "sense of history" so you have a feel for what came before. The more often you have a sense of de ja vu[35] in business, finance, and economics, the more opportunities you will spot and the fewer mistakes you will make.

I recommend anything sold by the bookstores listed under Constitutional law. An excellent book to start with is MAINSPRING OF HUMAN PROGRESS, by Henry Grady Weaver.

---

[35] Pronounced day-za-voo. The feeling that one has previously had an experience that is really new.

Also, history museums are one of the best sources of economic history. Although it is not generally recognized, in most cases history museums are about economic history, not political history. Top examples are the railroad museum in Sacramento, California, and Colonial Williamsburg in Virginia.

House Construction

House construction is another important field of knowledge; get a job building houses. Knowing how houses are built will be wonderfully helpful when it comes time to buy a house, or make repairs, or invest in real estate.

Equally important, you need to avoid being seen as an intellectual with no "real world" experience. The more jobs you've done where you've gotten your hands dirty, the more credible you will be in everything else you do.

Working as an apprentice for a small builder may teach you more than working for a large builder. In the interest of mass production, a large builder might restrict you to learning a few specialized tasks, while a small builder would be more likely to teach you the whole job, from digging the foundation to shingling the roof. Talk with the builder before you sign on.

It's been almost 25 years since I have built a house, and today I hire people to do all that kind of work for me. But knowing how houses are built and how repairs are done enables me to understand what repair persons are talking about and monitor the quality of the job they are doing.

Automobile Engines, Guns, Tools, Sports Equipment

Even if you don't like these subjects, learn enough about them to carry on an intelligent conversation. Being left out of a conversation is a sure ticket to being left out, period.

To learn about automobiles, befriend a mechanic or take a course.

For the others, spend time talking with people who know a lot about them. Most people enjoy teaching about their hobbies.

Football

Again, like it or not, this team-sport has become a model for the business world, which relies so much on teamwork. In football, each team member must do his job well or the play falls apart. The business world uses a lot of football metaphors — she scored a touchdown, he dropped the ball, we'd better punt. Learn this language.

Team Sports

Get into a team sport for a while (soccer, basketball, whatever) so you can learn the protocols[36] for teamwork.

The first time you play quarterback you will learn more about the real world than any five college courses will ever teach you.

---

[36] Protocols: rules of behavior. Formalities. Customs, especially in communication.

Personal Skills

Learn to smile and have an open, accepting manner

If you want people to approach you with opportunities, you must be approachable. To practice, be friendly with store clerks when you shop.

Learn to shake hands confidently

Few things in life are as important as first impressions. Your grip should be firm but not crushing, and dry, not sweaty. Ask an older person to teach you and practice with you. Which older person? Usually sales people who sell big-ticket items are good at handshakes; they know how important it is.

"Dress for Success"

Clothing, hair, cosmetics, etc. — style. You, and the product or service you sell, will create a first impression. No matter how good the product, its packaging must be first class or it will not sell well, so you and your product both need to "dress for success."

Even if you are not interested in contemporary fashion, you need to dress consistent with your career position and company's image. When I give a speech to a room full of millionaires, I'm as careful about choosing the right color tie as I am about selecting the right information.

Manners, Poise

First impressions again. Study the NEW COMPLETE GUIDE TO EXECUTIVE MANNERS, by Letitia Baldrige to help shape those first impressions.

Vocabulary

Chris, your intelligence will be judged more by your ability to speak (and your ability to write) the language than by any other factor including whatever college degrees you may have. Your reading and listening vocabularies should be as extensive as you can make them.

Your speaking vocabulary should be very simple and concise — all ten-cent words — but in your back pocket you should always have a collection of four-dollar words ready to pull out and use if you need to. But try to stick to those ten-cent words as much as possible.

No need to buy a vocabulary-building book, there are dozens of them in print at any given time, and the ones I have seen have all been pretty much the same. A librarian or English teacher should be able to steer you in the direction of a good one you can borrow from the library.

Meet People, Make Contacts, Network

The more people you know, and the more you help them, the more of them will help you.

One of the first organizations to check out is Junior Achievement, which teaches young people how to set up and operate businesses. At the time I write this, their URL is www.ja.org

Chris, one of the best things you can do to become successful is meet people who have already gotten to where you want to be, and listen to them. Be polite, but don't be bashful about asking questions. It is a big ego trip to be asked for advice, most of the time you will get plenty for free.

Try asking, "I notice you are very successful, what's the most important thing you've learned?" I am sure you will get thousands of dollars worth of advice at no charge.

Listening Skills, and Reading Body Language

Practice being a good listener, and read a book or two about body language so that you are sensitive to what others are feeling. One of the classics is HOW TO READ A PERSON LIKE A BOOK, by Gerard I. Nierenberg and Henry H. Calero. An understanding of body language can help you know when you are accidentally triggering cognitive dissonance so that you can back off before you create an enemy.

Debate

In a high school or college course, learn how to argue the pro and con of any subject. Be able to switch sides at the drop of a hat. This helps teach you reasoning skills and helps you learn to see things from the other person's point of view. It also helps you defend your point of view when you try to make a case for what you believe is right.

Chris, those are my suggestions for how to learn what you will need for success in your business, career, and investments. They naturally lead to the question, should you get a college degree?

I never argue against a degree. You do not know what life will bring your way, and having a college diploma is good insurance, if nothing else. It can help you get a higher paying job in case you ever need one.

Nothing is for sure; your business might go broke.

Chris, a college education also helps you know what goes on in college, and what does not. Most of the top decision-makers you will deal with for the rest of your life will have college degrees, and it helps to be part of this "in" crowd.

Do not expect a degree in business to be an automatic ticket to successful entrepreneurship. As I mentioned earlier, most business degrees are about getting executive jobs in large corporations, not starting and running your own firm.

In college you can learn a lot that will be useful, but, in my opinion, to be a successful entrepreneur you will also need the knowledge and skills I have suggested. Especially the selling skills, all businesses need to be able to sell.

Uncle Eric

23

How to Acquire a Business

Dear Chris,

To emphasize again, in my opinion, given economic conditions as I write this today, the strategy for success that has the best risk vs. reward ratio is to own a business. First follow my suggestions about how to be successful, then go out and get to work building your own business.

Chris, you may have heard the old saying, the first million is the hardest. It is amazingly true. I know a lot of millionaires, and they all tell essentially the same story. The first million was like climbing the Matterhorn[37]. The second was like climbing a low foothill. The third, and each one after that, was a speed bump.

The reason the third and later millions come so much more easily is, by the time an entrepreneur achieves the second million, he has found what works. He has a business model that makes money for him.

After the entrepreneur has her or his model, it is like owning a money machine. Turn the crank and money comes out. Turn the crank faster and more money comes out.

---

[37] A mountain in Switzerland.

The most difficult part is the start-up, the development of the model. Reaching your first million is the sign the model has been completed, or nearly so. The second million is evidence the model is up and running smoothly, most of the bugs have been worked out.

That is the hard way to get a business model.

The easiest, more reliable way is to buy a **franchise**.

The word franchise has several meanings. In the case we are speaking about here — that of a business model — a franchise is the right to buy and operate a business that has been developed by someone else. The franchiser sells the franchise to the franchisee. Usually, the franchisee pays a sum of money up front, then a monthly percentage of the income to the franchiser.

In other words, a franchise is a business model that is already through the development stage. You buy it from the people who invented it.

The most commonly cited example of a franchise is McDonalds®. There are thousands of others, few of which cost as much as a McDonalds®. Types of franchises are unlimited — hamburger stands, educational services, flower shops, cleaning services, windshield repair, plumbing, automobile oil changing, health food stores, coffee shops, and on and on. Go to the Internet and do a Google™ search for "franchise opportunities." Also try these web sites:

www.franchiseopportunities.com
www.franchisesolutions.com

To get started looking for a good franchise, first read Michael Gerber's books about the E-Myth. (You will find "E-Myth" in the titles.) Gerber explains how to avoid common problems that arise in running a business and how franchises work. I consider Gerber's guidance an absolute must.

Then contact the International Franchise Association: www.franchise.org, phone: 202-628-8000. The IFA offers a large quantity of books and reports about how to run a business successfully and how to choose a good franchise.

A franchise is not for everyone, but I do hope you will consider it, Chris. A franchise is a business model that already has a proven track record. It is designed to be easily duplicated. Save your money, buy one, and make it work. Save more money and buy another. Then another, and another.

Turn the crank and money comes out. Turn the crank faster...

As I write this, I have been walking around on this planet for almost sixty years, and this is the easiest, most reliable way I have seen to become a multimillionaire. Instead of building your own model from scratch, buy one already proven to work; then buy more.

Chris, I achieved my success the hard way, I invented my business model from scratch. It worked, but if I had it to do over again, I'd first give a franchise a try.

This is not to say there is anything wrong with building your own business from scratch — from developing your own model — many have done it and have become millionaires, or even billionaires. But it is the toughest way to go.

A very important point: one of the best things about a franchise is that, if you get a good one, it will be one in which the franchiser earns most of their money not from the sale of the franchise but as a percentage of the income generated by you. This means the franchiser has a mighty incentive to help you become successful. They will give you training and hold your hand while you are getting your new business up and running. And, the franchiser will be continually looking for ways to help the franchisee become more successful.

If you plan to go the franchise route, Chris, do not sign the purchase agreement until you have talked with several people who have owned a franchise of that type a long time, so that you know what you are getting into. Again, the materials offered by the IFA will be a big help. And, don't sign any legal contract without the assistance of a qualified attorney who has experience in franchise law.

Uncle Eric

24

What Kind of Millionaire Do You Want to Be?

Dear Chris,

During the 1990s, we saw a lot of bookstores pushing titles promising that you could get rich quick by investing in "dot-coms," meaning internet companies. Millions bought these stocks, but the dot-com get-rich-quick model did not work very well. By 2003, most of these investors had suffered enormous losses.

Now I am seeing books promising you can get rich quick in real estate. One says you can be a millionaire before your 27th birthday.

Most real estate strategies involve heavy "leverage," meaning borrowing a lot of money. This leads us to the subject of accounting.

Chris, accountants use this equation to show a person's financial condition, or balance sheet:

$$\text{assets} = \text{debts} + \text{net worth}$$

The assets are a person's holdings, or his estate, everything he controls. These include his income-producing possessions, such as his business and investments, as well as his consumer goods such as house and cars.

Debts help him acquire these assets, and the more debt he has, the more assets he can buy.

Net worth is the measure of his true wealth. If the net worth is $1 million, he is a millionaire. If two million or more, a multimillionaire.

Chris, if you could choose, would you like to have a net worth of $2 million, or $5 million?

I am sure most would say $5 million.

Consider two investors:

	Assets		Debts		Net Worth
Investor #1:	$100 million	=	$95 million	+	$5 million
Investor #2:	$2 million	=	0	+	$2 million

Now which investor would you like to be, the one who is worth $5 million, or $2 million?

Chris, I believe most investors, even those who know a lot about accounting and finance, would rather boast about a net worth of $5 million. Even more, they'd like to be able to boast about their $100 million estate.

$100 million versus $2 million. No contest, right?

Estate #1 is what I call the prestige estate; #2, the safe estate.

Investor #1 might feel more prestigious because of the greater assets, and might have more toys and gadgets and romantic opportunities, but if he (or she) makes a slip — if this person loses just 5% of his assets — his net worth is wiped out; he is broke and on the verge of bankruptcy.[38] His life can be paradise to purgatory at the drop of a hat.

The reason is that when you lose money, your debts remain. You are legally and ethically obligated to pay them even if you are broke. Not fun.

If investor #2 makes a 5% slip, not much happens — remember, this is the safe estate. Her (or his) $2 million net worth drops to $1.9 million, and her way of life remains unchanged, because she has no debt.

It has been my experience that people who get to be real estate millionaires before age 27 do it by building prestige-type estates. Mountains of debt.

Few of us ever divulge our balance sheets, so no one finds out that the investor with the big estate is really a slave to his debt. He does not own his estate, his estate owns him.

Here is another way to look at it, Chris. Stop a hundred people on the street and ask them, would you rather own a hot dog stand or a railroad?

I am sure not more than one or two would have the wisdom to ask, which one is making the most money?

Chris, would you rather own a hot dog stand that is earning money, or a railroad that is bankrupt?

Never judge a person's financial condition by the size of what he owns. Lots of people who look extremely wealthy are extremely broke. In many cases, they do not understand

---

[38] Bankruptcy: a condition in which a debtor cannot pay his debts; usually, a court declares the debtor bankrupt, then the people who loaned him money take his assets, or operate these assets to pay the debt. Bankruptcy is generally seen as an embarrassing failure because the person has violated his promises to pay his debts. He may be seen as untrustworthy.

enough about accounting to realize it. I often heard my father make the comment, "he's broke and doesn't know it."

Chris, I like freedom, and I like to be able to sleep at night, so my preference is for the safe estate, but what you choose is up to you. When making plans for your financial future, decide which kind of millionaire you want to be. Will it be the kind with a small estate that you own, or a large estate that owns you?

To help answer this question, determine what your personal risk tolerance is. Are you comfortable with risk? Or are you more comfortable playing it safe? A good book that helps young people and new investors understand about risk tolerance is THE YOUNG INVESTOR by Katherine R. Bateman.

Uncle Eric

P.S. I have given you a lot of suggestions for earning big money in the most low-risk, reliable way I know, by owning a good business. So, now that you know how to make money, my next few letters will explain how to keep it. Until then, here are four more books that will be useful to you.

CONSUMER REPORTS MONEY BOOK. This is about personal finance — stocks, bonds, interest rates, CDs, etc.

BARRON'S DICTIONARY OF BUSINESS AND FINANCE TERMS. In any field, knowing the language is half the battle.

START YOUR OWN BUSINESS, by Rieva Lesoksky & ENTREPRENEUR magazine. This book contains lots of ideas and insights about starting and operating a business.

THE MILLIONAIRE NEXT DOOR, by Thomas J. Stanley and William D. Danko. Profiles of people who have achieved financial success.

Chris, as I said in an earlier letter, looking back over my life I realize that if I had gone through this course of study early in life, I probably would have achieved success twenty years earlier than I did. It is too late for me, those twenty years are gone, but not for you, so I hope you will make a sincere effort to learn all you can about operating a successful business. Remember the remark by comedian George Burns: "I've been rich and I've been poor. Rich is better."

25

Savings and Investments

Dear Chris,

Use your business to earn money and your investments to keep the money. In this letter we begin looking at the threats to your savings. Then a few letters down the road, we will see how to overcome these threats.

My first rule for achieving financial success is, don't lose money.

Your planning should begin with this fact: studies show that for more than a century, the maximum low-risk "real" return you could expect on your investments has been 4%.

The real return is the return minus the rise in consumer prices. If consumer prices are rising at 3% and your savings account is earning 7% per year, your real return is 4% per year.

Chris, I know it seems ridiculously early for you to start planning for your retirement, and I'd be surprised if you did so with any seriousness, but much of what I will talk about now in regard to retirement will be useful in your early life. It will guide you toward decisions you will be glad you made when you are middle-aged and looking back at your youth.

To plan for your retirement, you should start with the question, how much income will I need after I retire?

List the cost of your expenses — taxes, insurance, food, medical care, rent, etc. — and total it up. This total is 4% of the "nest egg" you will need.

If your annual retirement income from investments needs to be $40,000, then your savings need to total $1 million plus your home. If you'll need $80,000, then your savings need to total $2 million plus your home.

There are not many jobs that pay enough to accumulate this much savings. This is a major reason I believe owning a good business is the most realistic way to become prosperous and stay that way.

At some point, you may find your $1 million nest egg earning, say, $100,000 because inflation has pushed up interest rates to 10%. In that case, for living expenses, a retiree would take out $40,000 plus, say, $4,000 to compensate for inflation, and plow $56,000 back into the nest egg to help make up for the money's loss of value from inflation. (You will understand more about this when you read my sets of letters about economics.)

Chris, this is extremely important: never assume you will be able to draw money from the nest egg itself. Any reduction in your savings reduces the ability of the savings to earn income, and you do not know how long you will live. If you run out of breath before you run out of money, fine; if you run out of money before you run out of breath, not fine.

These days, medical breakthroughs come so often that, in my opinion, someone who is middle-aged should plan to live until at least 100, and someone your age, 120. Since we cannot expect to be able to work past age 65 or 70, the middle-aged person should plan to be dependent on savings for at least 30 years. Someone your age, 50 years.

Thirty years? Fifty years?

Wow.

Again, this is a major reason I believe entrepreneurship is the only realistic route to success. The government is so big now, which means taxes are so crushing, that I cannot see a conventional wage-earning job generating enough savings.

A good business can be grown, almost without limit.

Let me emphasize, Chris, spending your savings today reduces the ability of your savings to earn income *for the rest of your life.*

I am the voice of experience.

In 1983, I thought I knew more than I did about a certain investment. I put $17,000 of my savings into it.

Bad move, I lost the whole $17,000.

Chris, that $17,000 was not really $17,000, it was $17,000 plus the interest I could have earned if I still had it.

Assuming the $17,000 had been put into tax-free municipal bonds in 1983, today that initial $17,000 would be worth $49,000.

It gets worse. The $17,000 lost in 1983 is $17,000 I will not have for the rest of my life. If we assume I will live another 40 years, and my bonds would earn an average 4% per year during this time, my lost $17,000 turns out to be a lost $235,000.

In other words, Chris, when I risked that $17,000 in 1983, I was really risking $235,000. And, I lost it, the whole $235,000.

Notice that risk decreases with age. If a person is only a year or two from meeting his Maker, the money he risks, or spends, is not worth much more than the face amount.

If he is young, the real value and risk are enormous; the money's ability to earn interest for fifty years or more could be lost.

This is why my first rule of finance is this: Don't lose money. A loss is always bigger than it appears on the surface.

And, the younger you are, the bigger the real loss will be.

So, Chris, whenever you are deciding to spend some of your savings, do the calculations — use a 4% real interest rate per year for the rest of your life — so that you know how much you are really spending.

In your last letter you said you plan to buy a new CD player. It will cost $89.00.

The price tag may say $89.00, but you are so young that the CD's real cost to you will be around $2,000.

Takes your breath away, doesn't it?

Now do you see why I say knowing about retirement planning can help you make wise decisions when you are very young?

What we are talking about here, Chris, is what economists call **opportunity cost**.

Opportunity cost means that no matter how you spend your time or money, you pay a price; you lose the ability to use that time or money for other things.

If you spend two hours playing baseball, then you cannot spend these two hours playing tennis, watching TV, or searching for a cure for cancer.

Spend $89 on your CD player now, and the day may come when you will not have your $2,000 to spend on a vacation in Paris or Tahiti.

Chris, opportunity cost is one of the most valuable concepts I ever learned, and I hope it will be as useful to you as it has been to me. A good rule of thumb: at your age, anything you buy costs you 22 times what the price tag says.

Uncle Eric

P.S. Chris, speaking of that 4% real interest rate, this is the maximum you can expect to earn with low risk. You might earn more by taking on more risk, but the risk rises quickly. At 5%, you might still be okay, but at 6%, the added risk is significant. At 7% it is sizable, and at 8% you are a riverboat gambler.

For the rest of your life you will hear pitches claiming that you can earn 100% or more. Some people do earn that much, no doubt about it. Some hit million dollar jackpots in Las Vegas casinos, too, but most who try it go home broke. If you are promised a real return of more than 5% per year, look out.

This does not apply to a business. It is common for a business owner to earn returns of 100% or more on invested money, but this is because the business owner is not trying to get rich without working. Business owners work very hard.

Chris, anytime someone says you can make big money without working, grab your wallet and run.

26

Social Security

Dear Chris,

Lots of people assume that because the government's Social Security system will send them a monthly check after they retire, they don't need to save as much as if they had to live entirely off their own nest egg.

That is a dangerous assumption.

The Social Security system works in a very simple way. Young people are forced to pay into it and retired people collect this money.

As long as the number of young people paying in is a lot greater than those receiving checks, the burden on the young is not too severe.

As the number of young shrinks, the burden on each taxpayer increases.

The people who are retired at the time I write this today experienced an astounding stroke of luck because of events that occurred after World War II ended in 1945. The soldiers returned home to their wives and these post-war couples started having babies, lots of them. This was the so-called Baby Boom that ran from 1945 to 1965.

The population of boomers is much larger than the population of their parents, so the tax burden on the boomers has been manageable.

But, that is where the good news ends. By the time the boomers were old enough to marry, the birth control pill had been invented; the boomers had fewer children. The Baby Boom was followed by the Baby Bust.

"Social Security is projected to founder under the burden of supporting the huge baby-boom generation," writes economist John Attarian; the number of workers supporting each beneficiary will "decline from 3.4 today to 2.1 in 2030."

Attarian reports that in 2017 Social Security will go into the red (will be losing more than it is earning) just as the boomers are starting to retire. To keep Social Security afloat, the government will need to take another seven *trillion* dollars in taxes on top of all the other taxes already being collected.[39]

It is not going to happen. There are not enough young people.

Anyone born after 1945 is taking a very big risk if they base their retirement planning on the assumption they will get a sizable amount of money from the government.

To be safe, Chris, assume the only money you will have to support yourself in retirement will be money you saved yourself.

Chris, do you really need that $2,000 CD player?

Uncle Eric

---

[39] "Social Security and its Discontents," by John Attarian, THE WORLD AND I, January 2003, p.251.

27

Real Estate and Debt

Dear Chris,

I am frequently asked about real estate as an investment.

Lots of people have earned fortunes in real estate, but most did it by treating their real estate not as an investment but as a business. It takes work.

The safest way to get into real estate is by saving your money and buying the property entirely with this money. This is called equity financing.

Many use debt financing. They borrow to buy the property.

The more you borrow, the more risk you are taking.

The larger the loan, the more you must earn to make payments on the loan. You can end up a slave to your estate.

Further, when a severe recession hits, and the value of your property, and income earned from it, declines, you must still make full payments on that debt. The payments do not go down.

More thoughts about real estate:

I need a place to live, so my home is not an investment and it will not appear in my investment plan unless I decide to sell it and live in a cardboard box. My home is consumption, same as my car and TV.

However, let's say I would be content living in a $100,000 home, and my present home is worth $300,000. I can consider $200,000 to be a real estate investment.

Real estate is surrounded by fallacies. One says you should buy land because "they aren't making any more of it."

The truth is that they are making more of it. Thanks to irrigation, roads, reclamation, and other methods, the amount of *usable* land has skyrocketed over the past century, and this trend will surely continue.

For instance, early maps of America labeled the area between Missouri and the Rockies as the Great American Desert. Today, corn, cattle, and condos cover 600,000 square miles of this "wasteland"

An eleven-story building increases the amount of surface area on which people can live or work tenfold.

All this newly usable surface area competes with existing surface area, including whatever surface area you and I might own.

The price of real estate as a category tends to rise, but this does not mean my particular parcel will.

Chris, I am not saying you should not own real estate, but real estate is not low risk, and never was.

On the other hand, bear in mind that when it comes to my hard-earned money, I am one of the most devout cowards you will ever meet. You may get a different view about real estate from persons who are more courageous than me.

But one thing I am certain about: If you are using debt to buy real estate — to buy anything — you are increasing your risk. Debt makes you inflexible. If you are chained to a big debt, you cannot get out of the way of an oncoming train.

I have met many sad people who passed up opportunities and stayed in dead-end jobs because they had to make payments on their debts.

This does not mean you should avoid debt in all cases, Chris, but be careful; debt is much more often an enemy than a friend.

Uncle Eric

28

Investment Advisors

Dear Chris,

While we are on the subject of investing, I should say a few words about investment advisors.

Advisors are necessary, and many are very helpful, in the same way that doctors and lawyers are helpful. Sometimes we need information from an expert who knows a lot more about a subject than we do.

However, it has been my experience that investment advisors are highly dangerous if you are trying to get rich. Because of my work as a geopolitical analyst, I have met hundreds of investment advisors, as well as stockbrokers and other financial specialists. Some appear to be wonderfully successful: wearing expensive tailored suits and gold and diamond jewelry, while traveling in chauffeured limousines.

Many of their clients assume these investment experts earned this money by investing.

As far as I have been able to tell, with only one or two exceptions, every investment expert I have met earned the bulk of his money from his business, not his investments.

A financial expert's primary job, like that of a doctor or lawyer, is to sell advice. He also may earn money by helping his clients get into investments, as in the case of stockbrokers. But, in my opinion, investment experts who have earned big money by investing are very rare.

Sometimes an advisor will make a buy that turns out very well, and he may tell you about it.

Being successful consistently over a period of, say, ten years is a different matter.

Some have done it, but this is what we would expect in a large population of any kind. This is because of something statisticians call the **bell-shaped curve.** A bell-shaped curve is a line on a chart in the shape of a bell. This curve appears almost everywhere; it is a crucially important model. Here is the story.

Chris, try this experiment. Have ten friends flip coins 100 times. Keep track of the results, heads and tails.

Will everyone get an exact 50-50 result, 50 heads and 50 tails?

Probably not. The results will cluster around 50-50, but most will probably be something like 48-52 or 45-55. One or two might be as far from the norm as 40-60.

Suppose you did the experiment with a million people, what result would you get then?

Again, on average, the results would cluster around 50-50, but with a population of a million, a few would be a great distance from the norm. One or two people might get 90 heads and 10 tails, and at the other end of the curve, one or two people might get 10 heads and 90 tails.

Measure horses by weight, or corn kernels by width, or lightning strikes by voltage, and in each study you will get this same kind of bell-shaped curve. Some measurements will be unusually large, some unusually small, and most will cluster around the average.

A Bell-Shaped Curve

Average Cases

Unusually
Low Cases

Unusually
High Cases

In any measurement of height, weight, income,
or anything else, including investment performance, most individuals will cluster around an
average. A few will be unusually high, and a few
unusually low.

Another experiment. At a party with 50 people, have
everyone flip coins, and track the results.

Someone will be an unusual case, way up at the high side
of the bell-shaped curve. Ask this person how he did it, "How
did you get 75 heads and only 25 tails?"

"I'm not sure, but while I was flipping the coin, I was
leaning against the wall chewing gum."

"Wow, that's amazing, let me try it. Were you leaning
like this, or like this? Did you have the gum in your left
cheek or your right?"

Some who know nothing about bell-shaped curves might
take you seriously and assume there is some connection

between gum chewing, wall leaning, and coin flipping. But you will know the 75-25 case was nothing to be surprised at, just luck, a natural result of the bell-shaped curve. The larger the population, the more unusual cases will appear, and the more extreme these unusual cases will be.

Chris, suppose, over a period of a year, 100 kindergarten children were handed the stock listings from the WALL STREET JOURNAL every day and asked to pick stocks. What result would you expect?

Again, a bell-shaped curve. At one end of the curve, you would have a few children doing much better than average, and at the other end, a few doing much worse. In the middle would be most of the children, clustering around the average.

Now suppose that instead of 100 children, you use 1,000 or a million. What results would you get?

You'd get another bell-shaped curve, with perhaps one or two children picking winners 80 or 90 percent of the time.

Would you put your own hard-earned money in the stock market, following these kindergartners' advice?

Notice this. Suppose you call the local newspaper to tell them about the amazing results these few unusual children produced. Also, suppose you do not tell the newspaper about the other million children.

The reporter, knowing only about these few winners, might do a front-page story about their amazing investment abilities.

This is what happens in the investment industry. With millions of people earning livings selling financial advice, there are always a few producing amazing results. They get a lot of publicity and their names are widely known throughout the industry.

Journalists ask these wizards about their secret techniques. "Mr. Stockpicker, what kind of technical analysis do you use? What kind of fundamental analysis? Which indicators do you watch?"

Did you do it by holding your gum in your left cheek, or your right?

Uncle Eric

29

Negative Real Interest Rates

Dear Chris,

On September 11, 2001, America entered another big war. The Pentagon expects the war to go on[40] at least until the year 2021, maybe even 2031, and I see no reason to disagree with that.

This is extremely important for saving money.

War can cause real interest rates to turn negative. When this happens, Chris, you are not earning enough on your savings to make up for the loss due to inflation, so the value (buying power) of your nest egg is shrinking.

Inflation is a hidden tax. The government prints dollars to pay for the war. The increase in the supply of dollars causes each individual dollar to lose value, so prices rise to compensate. The value lost by your money is the value covertly taken by the government. You will learn more about this in my set of letters called WHATEVER HAPPENED TO PENNY CANDY?

Chris, I did some research to learn the exact effect wars have had on real interest rates.

---

[40] "Pentagon Draws Up...," New York Times, 17 Jan 03.

The largest and longest U.S. wars of the 20th century were World War I, World War II, the Korean War, and the Vietnam War. Using databases from the Bureau of Labor Statistics, the Federal Reserve, and HISTORICAL STATISTICS OF THE UNITED STATES, I checked short-term interest rates and Consumer Price Index changes in all four wars.

Short-term rates mean rates for investments of one year or less.

I used short-term rates — U.S. Treasury Bill rates, these are the safest short-term instruments — because long-term instruments are grossly dangerous for savings during a period of serious inflation. You could invest dollars that are each worth one loaf of bread, and ten years later get back dollars that are worth one slice.

In all four wars, real interest rates went negative.

The least serious case was the Korean War. The worst year in that war was 1950, when real interest rates were a negative 4.5%. In other words, during 1950, the value, or buying power, of your savings would have shrunk about 4.5%. Prices were rising that much faster than interest rates.

Chris, bear in mind, this is a 4.5% loss in just one year.

The most serious case was World War I. In the worst year of that war, 1917, the government would have consumed 16% of your nest egg.

The longest period of negative real interest rates was the Vietnam War in which your savings would have taken a hit for seven years. The worst year in that war was 1974 in which the value of your nest egg would have shrunk 5%.

The worst year of World War II was actually the year after it ended, 1946, when price controls were lifted. In that one year alone, you would have lost over 17% of your savings. And 1941 was nothing to cheer about either, that year's loss was over 9%.

The sharpest, most severe drop was in the First World War. In just three years, prices rose so much more than interest rates that the value of a $1 million retirement fund was reduced to $659,000.

In short, Chris, if negative real interest rates go on for a long time, no amount of savings can be enough.

Will rates go negative in this new war? By the end of 2003 they already had. Will this continue? We cannot know, but history says that's the way to bet.

Incidentally, Chris, this analysis ignores the effect of income taxes. We are taxed on the advertised interest rate, not the real rate, so taxes make the losses much worse.

All we can say for sure is, the longer any war goes on, the more likely millions of savers will lose much of their nest eggs.

Chris, talk with someone old enough to remember previous wars. He or she probably knew retired people who were forced back to work, usually at low-wage jobs, because the value of their savings had been ravaged by the government's inflation.

What to do about it?

My next letter.

Uncle Eric

30

How to Keep
What You Have Earned

Dear Chris,

As I wrote in an earlier letter, use your business to earn money and your investments to keep that money.

For savers, the main problem during the 1990s was that highly safe Treasury-Bills and CDs were okay for an environment in which inflation was showing up in stock prices instead of consumer prices — consumer prices were rising at only one to three percent per year — but as of September 11, 2001, we are in a different ballgame.

One of the primary lessons from the more than 14,000 wars over the past 56 centuries is that big wars bring big inflations. As we saw in my previous letter, during severe inflations, T-Bills and CDs can be damaged by negative real interest rates.

After 9-11, I began worrying about this and began searching for a better way to save — a model for wartime.

The nearest thing I have found to a bulletproof investment model is the "Permanent Portfolio" plan taught by financial advisor Harry Browne.

The Permanent Portfolio plan is not 100% safe, but it is the safest thing I have seen, and it is the only plan I think has a prayer of surviving the turmoil of the 21st century without a big loss and without wide, frightening swings.

Wide swings are a highly important, but often overlooked, factor. We have all seen pitches that claim: Put your money in such-and-such because in the long run it always generates excellent profits.

Chris, the problem is that such-and-such usually takes wild, terrifying drops along the way. Drops sometimes last years or decades, and few investors have the courage to ride through them. I certainly don't.

So, in searching for a new, safer way to save, one of my prime requirements has been that the investment avoids wild swings. Browne's system has met this requirement throughout its 25-year lifespan, and I think it has an excellent chance of continuing to do so.

An easy way to follow the Permanent Portfolio plan is to first educate yourself about it by reading Browne's book FAIL-SAFE INVESTING — LIFELONG FINANCIAL SECURITY IN 30 MINUTES, which you can find on Browne's web site, www.HarryBrowne.org. Take some time to browse his site to acquaint yourself with his philosophy, his products, and his services.

Then consider Permanent Portfolio Fund (PRPFX, 800-531-5142), which uses the strategy. The mix in Browne's book is a bit different than that of PRPFX, but the results of PRPFX have been impressive. Conceived not to be a big profit-maker, but to give safety and stability in the face of serious trouble — to let you sleep at night — the Permanent Portfolio Fund is a mix: 15% real estate and natural resource stocks, 15% aggressive growth stocks, 35% U.S. Treasury bonds, 20% gold, 5% silver, 10% Swiss franc assets.

Note: the Permanent Portfolio is the *theory*, and Permanent Portfolio *Fund* is one way, the easiest way, to implement it.

The premise of PRPFX, which is a reflection of Browne's thinking, is that the future is not predictable, catastrophes will happen, but this mix can survive almost anything. In any given crisis, some parts of the fund will profit enough to offset losses in other parts.

You will find a truly amazing chart at Harry Browne's web site; type in:

www.HarryBrowne.org/PermanentPortfolioResults.htm

As you study it, think about the disasters that have hit the investment markets during the past 30 years. These have included the Vietnam War; the 1973 and 1979 oil shocks; recessions in 1974, 1980, 1982, 1991, and 2001; the Iran-Iraq war of the 1980s; the Soviet-Afghan war of the 1980s; the 1990-91 Bush-Hussein war; the collapse of the Asian Tigers in the mid-1990s; the great stock market crash at the end of the 1990s; and September 11th.

I do not know anything that has weathered these disasters as well as the Permanent Portfolio strategy.

Any given investment in the mix would be highly risky by itself, but the overall mix has been very strong. At any point in time, some investments have always done well enough to offset losses in those that were weak.

Chris, I do not know anything that has been as unfrightening as PRPFX in the face of all the turmoil since the end of the Cold War (in the early 1990s). The fund has had flat periods, but never a serious sustained decline, and most importantly, it had little reaction to September 11th.

I am not 100% confident about this model, but it is the best thing I have seen.

Internet URLs change constantly, but as I write this, you can see a chart of Permanent Portfolio Fund's performance by going to www.bigcharts.com. Type in PRPFX, and hit Interactive. When the interactive chart comes up, go to "time" and choose All Data.

Chris, a cardinal rule in finance is, diversify, diversify, diversify. I'm uncomfortable seeing you put all your money in a single mutual fund. So, I suggest you place between 25% and 50% of your eggs in the PRPFX basket, and invest the rest yourself directly according to the PRPFX mix, or something similar.

For additional diversification, Chris, I am comfortable with U.S. Savings Bonds. These have some inflation protection, so they are the safest U.S. paper investments you can own. I like the series EE best, but I also buy the series I.

In the inflation-protection model for the series EE, the interest rates are tied to the interest paid on five-year **Treasury securities**. During serious inflations, investors want to be compensated for the risk of having their money tied up, so they demand higher long-term interest rates. The series EE bonds earn interest tied to these higher rates.

In the inflation-protection model for the series I bonds, the interest rates are tied to the **Consumer Price Index**. This index tends to rise during serious inflations, but I do not trust the accuracy of the government's index as much as I trust the accuracy of interest rates. This is why the series EE bonds are my first choice.

Call around for a bank that sells Savings Bonds, and go to www.savingsbonds.gov for more information.

Chris, if you keep your money in the Permanent Portfolio plan and U.S. Savings Bonds, I think your savings have a good chance of surviving this new era of extreme turmoil.

Uncle Eric

31

Summary

Dear Chris,

You should now be ready to move on to my next set of letters called WHATEVER HAPPENED TO PENNY CANDY? But before doing so, I've summarized below the most important points we have covered so far.

Chris, none of this is an exact science, it is almost entirely my opinion, and I am sure that as I learn more I will be tweaking it for the rest of my life. My models are not perfect or complete; they are the best I can give you at this time.

1. Models are how humans understand their world. Models are so important to us that we are very reluctant to question them. When faced with a contradiction between data and a model, we almost always throw out the data, not the model.

2. Sometimes models are called paradigms (pair-a-dimes). When someone makes a big change to a model, or drops it altogether and adopts a new one, this is called a paradigm shift.

3. Because models are so important, we give a lot of care and attention to improving them. We are always trying to make them better, and this makes life easier for us.

4. One of the key uses for models is in sorting incoming information to decide what is important and what is not.

5. Models are rarely mentioned or explained in schools.

6. If you want to understand how the world works, and how to cope with it successfully, think in terms of learning good models. Facts are nice, but models are essential. When trying to learn something, start by asking for the model.

7. All of my letters to you, Chris, are based on a model that says there is a Higher Law than any government's law. In my set of letters called WHATEVER HAPPENED TO JUSTICE? you will learn about the two fundamental rules of this Higher Law.

8. The standard of proof we use to decide if something should be incorporated into our models is a personal choice. It depends on how important a model is to you. The more important the model, the higher should be your standard of proof.

9. On things that are important, we should continually ask, where is the evidence? Show me the evidence.

10. Whenever an expert confronts you, always look for the hidden agenda. If this person is trying to persuade you to do something, ask why? What's in it for him?

11. The less evidence you have for committing your money to something, the closer you are to outright gambling.

12. We have an inborn tendency to create models automatically, through experience. So do animals.

13. Stories about concrete examples create models automatically.

14. One of the most dangerous weaknesses in traditional education is that it contains no model for political history. Students are taught unconnected collections of facts — without any way to tie them together and make sense of them. When studying or teaching history, try this model: see history not in terms of rich vs. poor, or man vs. nature, but in terms of Higher Law vs. political power. You might find it makes more sense.

15. As a model for choosing models, and for discovering facts, the scientific method is not perfect, but it is hard to beat.

16. The key to the scientific method is the ability to predict. Does the hypothesis predict the results, and does it do so every time?

17. If you are not an expert in the field a model deals with, try to test the model against what you do know.

18. Beware of tautologies, or circular reasoning, in which a claim is used to prove itself.

19. The easiest way for a powerseeker to control a population is to convince people they have an obligation to behave according to his agenda. The easiest way to do this is to insert in their minds models that serve the agenda.

20. Cognitive dissonance is a form of stress that happens when a person encounters a fact or persuasive idea that disagrees with his model. The more important his model is to him, the greater will be his stress.

21. Beware of certainty. Certainty stops inquiry. Our models should be always under construction, never finished, and always open to question because we are human and humans make mistakes.

22. Bad models lead to bad behavior. When you see a good person being harmed, question the model held by the person doing the harm.

23. Material things are not the so-called good life, but they can help you get to the good life, and they can make it easier for you to help others. Effective models are the first requirement.

24. For most of history, there were two models for success. One was to work for a government. The other was to own a business. In the 20th century, a third model appeared; you could get into the upper middle class or affluent class by having a good job with a solid company. This can be called the prosperous employee model.

25. After 1970, the prosperous employee model began to fade. Some still make it work, but it gets more difficult every year.

26. When seeking entry-level jobs, regard them as courses of study. Select ones that teach valuable skills, and after you have learned all a job can teach you, move on to the next one.

27. The surest route to financial security is to develop good selling skills. These skills will not only help you sell goods and services, they will enable you to sell yourself when you are applying for jobs.

28. Consider getting a college degree. Life is uncertain, you never know what might be headed your way; your business might fail. Having a college diploma in your back pocket is good insurance, if nothing else. It can help you get a higher paying job in case you ever need one.

29. Before trying to invent your own business model from scratch, consider buying a franchise, which is a model that has already been proven.

30. Beware of debt. Debt can be useful, but it is also dangerous; it keeps you from being flexible, and each dollar of debt makes your financial condition more fragile.

31. Use your business to earn money, and your investments to keep that money.

32. Studies show the best low-risk "real" (adjusted for inflation) return you can expect on your investments is 4% per year; risks rise quickly above 4%. At 5%, you might be okay, but at 6%, the added risk is significant, and at 7%, sizable. At 8% you are a riverboat gambler.

33. Spending or losing money at a young age is much more expensive than during old age. A dollar given up at age 14, for instance, is a dollar that will not be able to earn income for you for 80 or 90 years, maybe more. A rule-of-thumb for a teenager is that anything you buy costs you 22 times what the price tag says.

34. Debt is more often an enemy than a friend.

35. When you see someone achieve amazing investment results, remember that millions of people participate in the investment markets. It is only natural that a few will, through luck, get results that are better than the norm, sometimes far better.

36. The new war that started September 11, 2001, blows hot and cold, but it could go on for decades; it will probably give us periods of negative real interest rates. This means inflation will probably reduce the buying power of your money faster than your money can earn interest. Consider the Permanent Portfolio plan and U.S. Savings Bonds as a way to protect against negative interest rates as well as against the other hazards of this new century.

Chris, we began this series of letters with your question: How can you achieve success in business, career, and investments? I hope you've found these detailed explanations useful. Now that you've read all these letters, you can see that the answer really boils down to just three rules:

1. Develop good models.

2. Never assume your models are complete; always continue refining them.

3. Keep an open mind, so you are always ready to consider new models.

In my next sets of letters you will begin learning models I have found to be useful. By the time you finish all my letters, I think you will find the collection of small models (the business model, economic model, legal model, and foreign policy model) beginning to merge into a single large one (Editor's note: "Uncle Eric's Model of How the World Works") which is fundamentally based on the two laws I will explain in WHATEVER HAPPENED TO JUSTICE?

Chris, this is not to say I am sure these models are correct, but they are the best I have found so far. I try very hard to apply rules 2 and 3, and I hope you will, too.

Chris, to repeat what I said at the conclusion of Part One, now that you understand models, you have an extremely useful tool that few others do. I look forward to hearing about the ways in which you use this tool, and I hope that you will share what you have learned with the people you care about.

Uncle Eric

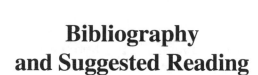

Bibliography
and Suggested Reading

(Check with your local library or favorite book store. At the time I write this, the titles that are asterisked are available through Bluestocking Press, web site: www.bluestockingPress.com or Phone: 800-959-8586.

• AIRBORNE by Tom Clancy, published by Berkley Publishing Group, 2000.

• ARMORED CAV by Tom Clancy, published by Berkley Publishing Group, 2000.

• BARRON'S DICTIONARY OF BUSINESS TERMS by Jack P. Friedman, Ph.D., published by Barron's Educational Series, 2000.

• BARRON'S DICTIONARY OF FINANCE AND INVESTMENT TERMS by John Downes, published by Barron's Educational Series, 1998.

• *THE BILL OF RIGHTS. Search the Internet.

• BLACK'S LAW DICTIONARY by Brian A. Garner, Editor, published by West Group, 1999.

• BLOWBACK by Chalmers Johnson, published by Owl Books, 2003.

• *BUSINESS MATHEMATICS by Miller, Salzman, Clendenen, distributed by Bluestocking Press, Phone: 800-959-8586 www.BluestockingPress.com

- *CAPITALISM FOR KIDS by Karl Hess, published by Bluestocking Press, Phone: 800-959-8586, web site: www.BluestockingPress.com

- CARRIER by Tom Clancy, published by Penguin, USA, 2000.

- THE COMPLETE IDIOT'S GUIDE TO U.S. SPECIAL OPS FORCES by Marc Cerasini, published by Alpha Books, 2002.

- CONSUMER REPORTS MONEY BOOK, by Janet Banford, published by Consumer Reports, 2000.

- *THE CONSTITUTION. Search the Internet.

- DIRTY LITTLE SECRETS: MILITARY INFORMATION YOU'RE NOT SUPPOSED TO KNOW by James F. Dunnigan and Albert A. Nofi, published by Quill, 1992.

- *ECONOMICS: A FREE MARKET READER, published by Bluestocking Press, Phone: 800-959-8586, web site: www.BluestockingPress.com

- THE ECONOMIST magazine. P.O. Box 58510, Boulder, CO 80323.

- THE E-MYTH by Michael Gerber, published by HarperCollins, 1988.

- FAIL-SAFE INVESTING — LIFELONG FINANCIAL SECURITY IN 30 MINUTES by Harry Browne, published by Griffin Trade Paperback, 2001.

- FIGHTER WING by Tom Clancy, published by Berkley Publishing Group, 2000.

- HANDBOOK OF EVERYDAY LAW by Gordon Coughlin, Jr., published by HarperResource, 1993.

- A HISTORY OF WARFARE by John Keegan, published by Vintage, 1994.

- *HOW TO LIE WITH STATISTICS by Darrell Huff, published by W.W. Norton & Co., 1954.

- HOW TO READ A PERSON LIKE A BOOK, by Gerard I. Nierenberg and Henry H. Calero, published by Pocket Books, 1990.

- HOW TO WRITE A GOOD ADVERTISEMENT — A SHORT COURSE IN COPYRIGHTING by Victor O. Schwab, published by Wilshire Book Company, 1985.

- *INTERMEDIATE ALGEBRA, by Margaret Lial, et al., distributed by Bluestocking Press, Phone: 800-959-8586 www.BluestockingPress.com

- *INTRODUCTORY ALGEBRA by Margaret Lial, et al., distributed by Bluestocking Press, Phone: 800-959-8586 www.BluestockingPress.com

- Knowledge Products audio history, published by Knowledge Products, Nashville, TN.

- LETITIA BALDRIGE'S NEW COMPLETE GUIDE TO EXECUTIVE MANNERS by Letitia Baldrige, published by Scribner, 1993.

- *MAINSPRING OF HUMAN PROGRESS by Henry Grady Weaver, published by The Foundation for Economic Education, Inc., 1953.

- MARINE by Tom Clancy, published by Berkley Publishing Group, 2000.

- THE MILLIONAIRE NEXT DOOR: THE SURPRISING SECRETS OF AMERICA'S WEALTHY by Thomas J. Stanley and William D. Danko, published by Pocket Books, 1998.

- THE OXFORD BOOK OF MILITARY ANECDOTES, edited by Max Hastings, published by Oxford University Press on Demand, 1986.

- *PLANNED CHAOS by Ludwig von Mises, published by The Foundation for Economic Education, Inc., 1947.

- THE PRINCE by Niccolo Machiavelli, published by Bantam, 1984. Penguin Classics edition translated by George Bull.

- *THE ROAD TO SERFDOM by F.A. Hayek, published by The University of Chicago Press, 1944.

- SHADOW WARRIORS: INSIDE THE SPECIAL FORCES by Tom Clancy, published by Berkley Publishing Group, 2003

- SPIN SELLING by Neil Rackham, published by McGraw-Hill Trade, 1988.

- START YOUR OWN BUSINESS by Rieva Lesoksky & Entrepreneur Magazine, published by Entrepreneur Media, Inc., 2001. This book contains lots of ideas and insights about starting and operating a business.

- SUBMARINE by Tom Clancy, published by Bt Bound, 2003.

- SUPPLYING WAR by Martin van Creveld, published by Cambridge University Press, 1979.

- *UNCLE ERIC'S MODEL OF HOW THE WORLD WORKS by Richard J. Maybury, published by Bluestocking Press, www.BluestockingPress.com; Phone: 800-959-8586. Book titles in this series include:

    UNCLE ERIC TALKS ABOUT PERSONAL, CAREER, AND
        FINANCIAL SECURITY
    WHATEVER HAPPENED TO PENNY CANDY?
    WHATEVER HAPPENED TO JUSTICE?
    ARE YOU LIBERAL? CONSERVATIVE? OR CONFUSED?
    ANCIENT ROME: HOW IT AFFECTS YOU TODAY
    EVALUATING BOOKS: WHAT WOULD THOMAS JEFFERSON
        THINK ABOUT THIS?
    THE MONEY MYSTERY
    THE CLIPPER SHIP STRATEGY
    THE THOUSAND YEAR WAR IN THE MIDEAST
    WORLD WAR I: THE REST OF THE STORY AND HOW IT AFFECTS
        YOU TODAY
    WORLD WAR II: THE REST OF THE STORY AND HOW IT AFFECTS
        YOU TODAY

- *THE YOUNG INVESTOR by Katherine R. Bateman, published by Chicago Review Press, 2001. Distributed by Bluestocking Press, Phone: 800-959-8586 www.BluestockingPress.com

- VIETNAM, A HISTORY: THE FIRST COMPLETE ACCOUNT OF THE VIETNAM WAR by Stanley Karnow, published by Penguin USA, 1997.

Glossary

AGENDA. A plan. A list of things to be dealt with or to do.

ALCHEMY. A forerunner of chemistry in the Middle Ages. Alchemists chiefly aimed to find a way to turn lead and other base metals into gold, to find a universal remedy for disease, and to find a way to prolong youth.

AUSTRIAN ECONOMICS. The most free-market of all economic models, and the one that is most in agreement with the ethical principles on which America was founded. Austrian economics sees the economy not as a machine (as other economic models do) but as an ecology made of biological organisms — humans.

BELL-SHAPED CURVE. A line on a chart in the shape of a bell. This curve appears almost everywhere; it is a crucially important model.

BRITISH COMMON LAW. The principles on which America was founded were those of the old British common law. The system for discovering and applying the Natural Laws that determine the results of human behavior. The body of definitions and precedents growing from the two fundamental laws that make civilization possible.

Underlying the common law are two basic rules. These rules are the point at which all religions intersect, the point on which all agree. Common to all religions, these laws were the foundation of the old common law. These two laws are: 1) do all you have agreed to do, and 2) do not encroach on other persons or their property.

CAPITALISM. Today capitalism is generally taken to mean free markets, free trade, and free enterprise.

CIRCULAR REASONING. A statement that uses itself to prove itself.

COGNITIVE DISSONANCE. The emotional stress that occurs when a person encounters a fact or persuasive idea that disagrees with his or her model.

CONSUMER PRICE INDEX. The federal government's measure of changes in prices of items purchased by consumers.

DICTATOR. A ruler with power on which there are no legal limits; the ruler can legally do anything he pleases to anyone.

DICTATORSHIP. A country under the control of a dictator.

ECOLOGY. As it relates to the economy, the highly complex interrelationships among people.

ECONOMICS. The study of the production and distribution of wealth.

ECONOMY. System for producing and distributing wealth.

ENTREPRENEUR. One who owns and operates a business.

EVIDENCE. Something that tends to prove.

EXPERT. A person who is highly knowledgeable about a subject.

FALLIBLE. Liable to make mistakes.

FRANCHISE. The right to buy, sell, and operate a business developed by someone else.

GEOPOLITICS. World political events, as opposed to domestic or national political events. Global politics. Relations among nations, as well as within nations.

GOVERNMENT-CONTROLLED SCHOOLS. Schools in which the lessons taught are strongly influenced or fully controlled by government agencies.

GOVERNMENT'S LAW. A law made up by human lawmakers.

GUERRILLA TACTICS. A very informal sort of warfare in which the soldiers are acting mostly in small groups or alone, on their own initiative. They are not uniformed and are not employed by a government. Their style is mostly hit-and-run. Higher Law: A law higher than any human law.

"HARD" SCIENCES. Usually physics and chemistry, and sciences derived from them. Sciences in which measurements can be extremely precise and in which we can have great confidence about the findings. Hard sciences can predict with great accuracy.

HIGHER LAW. A law higher than any human law.

INDUSTRIAL REVOLUTION. Beginning in the 1700s, the change from hand tools to large machines, power tools and factories that made goods and services much less expensive due to mass-production.

INVESTMENTS. Bank accounts and other places to put savings in hopes of earning more money.

JANISSARY. A soldier in the Turkish sultan's personal guard and army, raised from childhood to be completely loyal and unquestioning of orders.

JOINT STOCK COMPANY. A joint stock company is like a very large partnership. Each owner has shares of stock (certificates of ownership) in the company and, like a partner, is fully responsible for whatever might go wrong.

LIBERTY. Protection of the individual's right to his or her life, freedom, and property. Widespread obedience to the two fundamental laws that make civilization possible: 1) do all you have agreed to do, and (2) do not encroach on other persons or their property.

LIMITED LIABILITY. Means the investor's risk is limited to the amount of his investment.

LIMITED LIABILITY CORPORATION. Like joint stock companies, thousands or millions can own a limited liability corporation (LLC). But unlike a joint stock company, each owner is responsible only for the amount of his investment, and can lose only that amount.

MILITIA. A part-time army composed of citizens, as opposed to full-time professional soldiers. The military equivalent of a volunteer fire department.

MINUTEMEN. In the American Revolution, a soldier who volunteered to be ready to fight at a minute's notice.

MODEL. Paradigm. A mental picture of how the world works.

MOUNTAIN CHART. In finance, a chart that shows a rising line, indicating profits, with no serious downturn.

NAZI. Member of a German fascist party controlling Germany under Adolf Hitler from 1933 to 1945.

NUREMBERG TRIALS. Trials held after World War II in the German city of Nuremberg to judge the guilt or innocence of Axis leaders.

OPINION. A belief that is not completely certain.

OPPORTUNITY COST. Opportunities lost when time or money are dedicated to something that prevents the time or money from being used in other ways.

PARADIGM. Model.

PARADIGM SHIFT. Extensive alteration of a model, or replacement of an old model with a new one.

PARTNERSHIP. A partnership is the same as a sole proprietorship, except that more than one person owns it. These people share the profits and the responsibilities

PORTFOLIO. A collection of investments.

POWERSEEKER. One who wishes to acquire the means to forcibly control others.

PRICE. The money or other valuable item traded for something.

PROSPEROUS EMPLOYEE MODEL. The 20th century condition under which a person working as an employee could enjoy comforts, conveniences, and financial security much greater than almost anyone before the 20th century.

SCHOOL OF HARD KNOCKS. Experience, as opposed to academic study. Usually experience containing many painful incidents.

SCIENTIFIC METHOD. The system of gathering, examining, testing, and proving evidence in support of a theory.

SET-PIECE BATTLES. This term has several definitions, depending on which military expert is using it. In this book, it means a battle in which the forces are all uniformed soldiers paid by one government or the other, with the forces arrayed on a battlefield against each other. A very formalized sort of warfare in which fortifications and firepower are more important than stealthy maneuvering.

"SOFT" SCIENCE. A field of study in which measurements are typically not very accurate, and in which we may not be at all confident about the findings. Soft sciences cannot predict with much accuracy.

SOLE PROPRIETORSHIP. Only one person owns a sole proprietorship. This person receives all the profits and bears all the responsibility.

STANDARD OF PROOF. Rules for judging truth.

STATISTICS. Facts stated as numbers, for the purpose of comparison or other analysis.

TAUTOLOGY. A statement that is logically correct but contains no useful information.

TREASURY SECURITIES. Treasury Notes, Treasury Bills, and Treasury Bonds. Debts owed by the Federal government to persons who have lent the government money by buying these instruments.

TRIVIA. Small, unimportant facts.

WISDOM. According to Webster's 1828 Dictionary, wisdom is "the right use of exercise of knowledge; the choice of laudable ends, and of the best means to accomplish them. This is wisdom in act, *effect*, or *practice*. If wisdom is to be considered as a *faculty* of the mind, it is the faculty of discerning or judging what is most just, proper and useful, and if it is to be considered as an *acquirement*, it is the knowledge and use of what is best, most just, most proper, most conducive to prosperity or happiness. Wisdom in the first sense, or *practical wisdom*, is nearly synonymous with *discretion.* It differs somewhat from *prudence,* in this respect; *prudence* is the exercise of sound judgment in avoiding evils; *wisdom* is the exercise of sound judgment either in avoiding evils or attempting good. *Prudence* then is a species, of which wisdom is the genus."

WORKING HYPOTHESIS. A belief taken as fact until it is proven wrong.

About Richard J. Maybury

Richard Maybury, also known as Uncle Eric, is a world renowned author, lecturer and geopolitical analyst. He consults with business firms in the U.S. and Europe. Richard is the former Global Affairs editor of MONEYWORLD and widely regarded as one of the finest free-market writers in America. Mr. Maybury's articles have appeared in THE WALL STREET JOURNAL, USA TODAY, and other major publications.

Richard Maybury has penned eleven books in the Uncle Eric series. His books have been endorsed by top business leaders including former U.S. Treasury Secretary William Simon, and he has been interviewed on more than 250 radio and TV shows across America.

He has been married for more than 35 years, has lived abroad, traveled around the world, and visited 48 states and 40 countries.

He is truly a teacher for all ages.

Index

Richard J. Maybury's
Uncle Eric Books

Review Comments or Endorsements
about Current or Previous Editions of the Uncle Eric Books

"This book [WHATEVER HAPPENED TO PENNY CANDY?] is must reading for children of all ages. Its presentation of some of the fundamentals of economics is lucid, accurate and above all highly readable."
                              —Michael A. Walker, Executive Director
                    The Fraser Institute, British Columbia, Canada

"Probably the best short course in economics around and is more valuable than a college text that's ten times its length. Buy a dozen and give them to friends. This is a great book!"   **—Douglas Casey, Author**
                              CRISIS INVESTING and STRATEGIC INVESTING

"Maybury's forte is explaining economics in an interesting, logical and easy-to-understand manner — no small achievement in economics pedagogy. Equally important, the economics in WHATEVER HAPPENED TO PENNY CANDY? makes such good sense. When government's economic policies make us say 'uncle' let's hope it's 'Uncle Eric', Maybury's letterwriter and alter ego."   **— John G. Murphy, Ph.D., President**
                    National Schools Committee for Economic Education, Inc.

"This [WHATEVER HAPPENED TO JUSTICE?] is a wonderfully readable and interesting book about the legal principles which undergird a free society. Richard Maybury challenges the reader to explore the inextricable connections between law and economics, and between economic and political liberty. I can think of no more important subject, and I highly recommend this lucid and thoughtful volume."   **—William E. Simon**
                              Former U.S. Treasury Secretary

"There is something revolutionary about the clarity of Mr. Maybury's explanations — his insight into Germany's prosperity and the method by which it was consciously achieved has the most profound implications for our own economic policy, which is also a deliberate construct. Hurray for PENNY CANDY! A brilliant book."   **—John Taylor Gatto, Author**
                              DUMBING US DOWN
                    New York State Teacher of the Year

"WHATEVER HAPPENED TO JUSTICE? is critical reading for all Americans. If our economic and political downfall is to be avoided, we must expose an entire generation of Americans to the ideas found in this wonderful book."
                              —Ron Paul, member of Congress

"Richard Maybury's WHATEVER HAPPENED TO JUSTICE? should be required reading for all who hold or aspire to hold public office, as well as for all members of the judicial system. It is a fitting companion volume to his earlier, WHATEVER HAPPENED TO PENNY CANDY?"   —**William Snavely**
Professor Emeritus of Economics
George Mason University

"There is a naked clarity to Maybury's thought that washes over the reader like cleansing rain. His examination of the dynamics of common law is brilliant. As a teacher for all ages, Mr. Maybury is a virtuoso. Bravo!"   —**John Taylor Gatto**
Former New York State Teacher of the Year

"If I were to recommend ten great books to introduce people to the most important issues facing our nation today, WHATEVER HAPPENED TO PENNY CANDY? and WHATEVER HAPPENED TO JUSTICE? would be high on my list."
—**Kevin J. Price, American Economic Foundation**

"While Maybury's 'lessons' are valuable for everyone, I especially recommend [THE CLIPPER SHIP STRATEGY] to potential entrepreneurs and businessmen. I would make it required reading for them if I could. (Those who might be employees can also find out how to select a career and/or company to work for that is likely to remain economically healthy!)...You might not agree with all of Maybury's suggestions, but after reading it, I expect you will know more about the way business really works than many business college graduates."   —**Cathy Duffy, Author**
CHRISTIAN HOME EDUCATORS' CURRICULUM MANUAL

"Richard Maybury is a great author! In his two-volume world war series, WORLD WAR II along with the companion volume WORLD WAR I, Maybury will give you a new perspective on wars and history, filled with facts of interest rarely mentioned elsewhere. 'Uncle Eric' writes succinctly and in a way to be understood. Highly, highly recommended.!"
—**Jim Cox, author,** THE CONCISE GUIDE TO ECONOMICS
Associate Professor Georgia Perimeter College

"The best book I've read on World War II. It provides genuinely original insights on why the U.S. didn't need to become involved, and destroys many myths that persist about the war. Maybury ties the misunderstandings about World War II to the misunderstandings about today's U.S. foreign policy. I also strongly recommend his books WORLD WAR I and WHATEVER HAPPENED TO JUSTICE?   —**Harry Browne**
WORLD NET DAILY

"The quality of the writing and information presented is exceptional."
—EDUCATIONAL OASIS (Good Apple)

Study Guides
available (or forthcoming)
for the Uncle Eric books

Each study guide will include some, and at times all, of the following:

1) Chapter-by-chapter comprehension questions

2) Research activities

3) A list of films

4) Thought questions

5) Final exam

Order from your favorite book store or direct from the publisher, Bluestocking Press.

Visit the Bluestocking Press web site at:

www.BluestockingPress.com

(See contact information
for the publisher, Bluestocking Press,
on the last page of this book.)

Bluestocking Press

Bluestocking Press publishes the following:

1) Richard J. Maybury's Uncle Eric books

2) CAPITALISM FOR KIDS by Karl Hess

3) BUSINESS: IT'S ALL ABOUT COMMON SENSE by Kathryn Daniels and Anthony Joseph

3) LAURA INGALLS WILDER AND ROSE WILDER LANE HISTORICAL TIMETABLE by Jane A. Williams

4) BLUESTOCKING PRESS CATALOG for children and adults. The catalog focuses on history, law, economics, entrepreneurship, and math . Product selections vary, and may include: primary source material, audio history, historical fiction, historical toys, historical music, and historical documents.

Visit the Bluestocking Press web site at:

www.BluestockingPress.com

For a printed catalog, contact Bluestocking Press.

(See contact information
on the last page of this book.)

Published by Bluestocking Press

Uncle Eric Books by Richard J. Maybury

UNCLE ERIC TALKS ABOUT PERSONAL, CAREER & FINANCIAL SECURITY

WHATEVER HAPPENED TO PENNY CANDY?

WHATEVER HAPPENED TO JUSTICE?

ARE YOU LIBERAL? CONSERVATIVE? OR CONFUSED?

ANCIENT ROME: HOW IT AFFECTS YOU TODAY

EVALUATING BOOKS: WHAT WOULD THOMAS JEFFERSON THINK ABOUT THIS?

THE MONEY MYSTERY

THE CLIPPER SHIP STRATEGY

THE THOUSAND YEAR WAR IN THE MIDEAST

WORLD WAR I: THE REST OF THE STORY

WORLD WAR II: THE REST OF THE STORY

Bluestocking Guides (study guides for the Uncle Eric books)
by Jane A. Williams and/or Kathryn Daniels

Each Study Guide includes some or all of the following:

1) chapter-by-chapter comprehension questions and answers
2) application questions and answers
3) research activities
4) essay assignments
5) thought questions
6) final exam

More Bluestocking Press Titles

LAURA INGALLS WILDER AND ROSE WILDER LANE HISTORICAL TIMETABLE

CAPITALISM FOR KIDS: GROWING UP TO BE YOUR OWN BOSS by Karl Hess

ECONOMICS: A FREE MARKET READER edited by Jane Williams & Kathryn Daniels

BUSINESS: IT'S ALL ABOUT COMMON SENSE by Kathryn Daniels & Anthony Joseph

The Bluestocking Press Catalog

Varied and interesting selections of history products: historical toys and crafts, historical documents, historical fiction, primary sources, and more.

Order information: Order any of the above by phone or online from:

Bluestocking Press
Phone: 800-959-8586

email: CustomerService@BluestockingPress.com

web site: www.BluestockingPress.com